P9-CIS-842
Panama City
Fla. 7/88

HOW TO MAKE CLIPPER SHIP MODELS

Loch Torrens, complete in Case on Stand

***Frontispiece*]**

How to Make
Clipper Ship Models

A Practical Manual dealing with every aspect of
Clipper Ship Modelling from the Simplest
Waterline Types to Fine Scale Models
fit for Exhibition purposes

BY

EDWARD W. HOBBS, P.A.I.N.A.

Vickers Gold Medallist

Author of "How to Make Old Time Ship Models"

GLASGOW

BROWN, SON & FERGUSON, LTD.

52 Darnley Street

First Edition - - 1927
Second Edition - - 1938
Reprinted - 1948, 1952, 1960
Revised - - - 1968
Revised Edition - 1971
Reprinted - - - 1975

Printed and Made in Great Britain

PREFACE.

IF you know aught of the sea or ships, if you love them but know little, if you would taste the salt brine on your lips, if you would venture across boundless waters, come with me, open the door to your dreams and make for yourself a little ship. But come with the right spirit, determined to make a model that calls back the good old sailing days, that brings to your ears the song of the wind and sea. Surely you have seen a model resplendent in silver and gilt, exquisitely built and finished but inanimate, a model that never by any chance could weigh anchor and slip away from its case at night to sail the seven seas and returning at daybreak await disdainfully the unseeing eyes of the visitors. Let your model become a living thing, a dream ship come true, a ship with all the mystery of the sea, redolent of empurpled nights in the tropics, of spice laden airs in the Indies, of storm and tempest in the roaring forties. Then shall your work be well begun and being so shall end well and your craftsmanship remain a tribute to your self and your work a joy to all.

This book is intended to show the novice how to make worth-while models of clipper ships, models with the Spirit of the Sea in them. The Author is no seafaring man, but for close on thirty years has known, made and loved models of ships of every kind. Probably the old salt—and the young ones too!—will chide because a rope is awry here or something out of order there! but perhaps they will kindly remember that this work is not intended as a treatise on Rigging—nor a history of clipper ships—but an endeavour to show how anyone can make really good clipper ship models, models that look like ships even if they are not meticulously accurate in each detail of every rope and tackle.

How many old seamen who are still left with us and have sailed on clipper ships have made notes, prepared sketches or models, or possess authentic illustrations of their ships? Perhaps if they knew the difficulties of ascertaining the needed information for rigging a particular ship model, they would be less prone to fulminate at the errors they may see in contemporary work, and would aid the cause of knowledge by giving from their own store! The Author would indeed welcome any constructive criticism of this nature, and endeavour to answer any questions within his power, either on clipper ships in general, or particularly to elucidate any difficulties which may confront the ship modeller.

This book is arranged progressively, and commences with a very simple waterline model of *Cutty Sark*, then goes on to explain the construction of a scenic model, and deals at great length with every detail of a complete scale model four master. The great number of specially prepared photographs showing the work in progress should prove invaluable to the novice, while all requisite working drawings are included in the text, or given in the large folding plates which are a feature of this book.

The Author tenders grateful and appreciative thanks to many kind friends for their assistance, to Messrs. Bassett-Lowke Ltd. of London, Northampton and Edinburgh, for permission to reproduce photographs of the model of *Cutty Sark*, and a selection of their ship model fittings, and to Messrs. Brown, Son & Ferguson, Glasgow, for their courtesy and care in the production of the book and for the loan of some illustrations in Chapter XVI.; also to the Director of the Science Museum, South Kensington, London, for permission to reproduce the illustrations of some models in the Museum (figs. 2 to 6) and finally to Miss Ethyl Smith for her painstaking work in preparing many of the details for the photographs so ably taken by my friend and collaborator Mr. S. W. Hodgkinson.

EDWARD W. HOBBS,
Past Assoc. Inst. Naval Architects.

LONDON, S.W.1, 1927.

PREFACE TO SECOND EDITION.

THAT the making of ship models—as a hobby or for industrial purposes is in no wise on the wane—is exemplified by the numerical increase in the numbers of such models, and by the steadily growing numbers of amateurs who find in this fascinating hobby a welcome relaxation from the strain of modern life, and withal a practical outlet for the ingrained human urge to make something.

To the Author and to the Publishers it has been most gratifying to receive numerous letters of appreciation from readers of the first edition of this work who have found it of practical service; in many cases, readers with no previous experience of ship modelling have succeeded at the first attempt in making pleasing and satisfactory models, and have followed up their initial successes by building models of other vessels, often of mediæval and early types such as are described in the companion work entitled *How to Make Old Time Ship Models.*

Not only is it satisfying to know from readers of their success, but it is also a matter for pardonable pride that the subject matter, its mode of presentation, and the meticulous care put into every phase of the text—together with the very large number of detailed working drawings and action photographs—have proved their sterling worth by the acid tests of time and experience.

No doubt the fact that every part and every constructional method described in this book was first tried out and tested in every way, and the actual models built specially for the purpose, has had much to do with the success of the book and the service it has already rendered to readers in all parts of the world.

For these reasons, it has been found unnecessary—and undesirable—either to add to, or to amend, the original matter, and this, the second complete edition, is unhesitatingly commended to all in search of proven and reliable information on one of the most delightful of modern hobbies—the modelling of clipper ships.

EDWARD W. HOBBS.

LONDON, *January*, 1938.

TIMES CHANGE

THIS book, first published in 1927, has survived many changes: a world war, vast technological progress, the widespread use of new materials, changes in the currency and the introduction of metrication.

But like vintage cars, and the vanishing Clipper Ships, interest therein increases with the passage of time and in both finds expression in models.

With such thoughts in mind, I had to decide either to extensively amend the original text and illustrations by substituting references to contemporary materials and processes, or to adhere to the well-established procedure dealt with in the original work and proved by the success of innumerable readers.

I decided to leave the work in the original form, retaining the names of men and firms, some of whom are no longer with us, but whose efforts did so much to make possible the production of the models described in this book and whose craftsmanship will remain for all time a gracious guide to those who follow.

Of the modern materials, sheet plastic and fibre glass generally require a mould whereon to form, for example, a boat hull; strips of plastic do not bend in such an agreeable way as wood for plank built models; but numerous small fittings could be machined from solid blocks or fabricated by building up from separate pieces.

The newer adhesives are admirable in many ways, for example, a brand of Araldite is useful in substitution for soldering many small metal parts.

The newer paints and synthetics, admirable for domestic purposes, are usually too thick to give the required delicacy of finish in small models.

Monetary references in the book have been left as indications of cost in 1927—everyone knows that the costs have risen enormously since then and are likely to continue to rise.

Similarly, all dimensions have been left in their original Imperial designations; it seems illogical to make models to metric dimensions when the originals and the ships themselves were built to Imperial dimensions. Anyone preferring the metric sizes can refer to the innumerable reference tables of equivalents and apply them accordingly.

Finally, a word in favour of some inexpensive electric power tools, such as the circular saw, sander and polisher, drill, and others, which save a lot of hard work in the formative and finishing stages of modelling.

But after all is said and done, in ship modelling the way of the old craftsmen is still by far the best way.

EDWARD W. HOBBS.

CONTENTS.

ILLUSTRATIONS.

PLATES.

How to Make Clipper Ship Models.

CHAPTER I.

INTRODUCTION—FAMOUS CLIPPERS.

Brief Description of Clipper Ships and Their Performances, Together with Notes on the Part they have Played in the Development of Empire. Illustrated with 6 Full-Page Photographs of Fine Clipper Ship Models.

AN hundred and fifty feet of canvas towering above us, the gleeful song of the wind in the shrouds, the swish and surge of ocean, and beneath our feet the gleaming decks, the steady heart pulse of a gallant ship at sea.

Roaming the world to distant parts, carrying the old flag to new lands, adding to the Empire, it was life, a life where man with bits of wood and canvas harnessed elemental forces with a rope, and most times won out by sheer grit and persistence.

They were days when men were men, quick and coarse of speech and jest, stern and enduring—hard bitten, tough, and weather worn—but men, and Britons at that! above all seamen. Work to be done was done with brawn and muscle, with gasping breath and heaving chest, eyes asmart with brine, hands torn and bleeding battling with iron-hard sailcloth and relentless wind. At times idling away the golden hours with merry song and jest, blithesome of heart—"For we are homeward bound, my boys—we are homeward bound."

FIG. 1.—Model of *Cutty Sark* built by Messrs. Bassett-Lowke, Ltd.

FIG. 2.—Model of Early China Clipper, rigged in the Science Museum, South Kensington, London.

Alas! the good old sailing ships are gone—gone as if ashamed of the animated iron boxes that nowadays do service as ships. Granted these oleaginous monsters are comfortable, speedy and reliable, but where are the old vitality, the old song in the blood, the stirring stateliness of the full-rigged ship, the grace and beauty of the clipper? Here and there in odd ports and out of way corners of the ocean a clipper glides by in a travesty of her old pride, soon to be hull down on the horizon, lost again in the mists of time.

Many of these gallant clippers conveyed emigrants to golden climes, to fortune or a pioneer's grave. Now they are nothing but a memory cherished by ageing shellbacks, their portraits in early oils or mezzotints lovingly stored in collectors' galleries, their timbers rotting in a thousand seas, they lie unhonoured in nameless graves—but their soul goes on for ever, for they were of the sea, and the sea is eternal!

Despite the advance of steam, electricity, and oil, despite the passing of three generations, we still love and admire the old clippers, we bow to the inevitable march of progress but always in the heart and mind of Britain the sailing ship remains the undisputed Queen of Ocean, the secret love of Britons, the symbol of sea service.

What wonderful passages were made by those old clippers, speeds that would be creditable to a modern liner were common. *Thermopylae*, for instance, ran from London to Melbourne in 60 days; *Sir Lancelot*, built at Greenock in 1865, completed the voyage from Foochow to the English Channel in 89 days.

Cutty Sark made a magnificent passage of 1050 miles in three days; the *Melbourne*, with a fine run of 374 miles in a day to her credit, averaged 82 days outward bound from London to Melbourne for something like twelve years. These names and speeds that come to mind are typical of hundreds of gallant ships whose records can be gleamed from such books as the *China Clippers*, *Colonial Clippers*, *Log of the Cutty Sark* and other works.

Not all the old clippers are lost; some are still afloat, and

Fig. 3.—Model of *Stonehouse* built in 1871

FIG. 4.—Fully rigged model of *Sudbourne*.

in particular, the gallant little *Cutty Sark*, sunning herself off Falmouth in new and fine clothes, saved from ignominious decay by loving hands; long may she remain to queen it as a gracious Lady of the Sea, scarred and weary but proud of her unbroken record as one of the fastest sailing ships the world has ever known.

Built at Dumbarton by Scott & Co. in 1869, a model of her, recently supplied by Bassett-Lowke Ltd., is shown in fig. 1, and a tribute to the skill of the celebrated ship modellers of Northampton. This model to a scale of $\frac{1}{4}$ inch to 1 foot is based on photographs and particulars derived from the actual ship; other photos of her appear elsewhere in this book.

A model of an early China clipper built about 1850 is shown in fig. 2; she was rigged in the workshops of the Science Museum, South Kensington, London, from particulars supplied by Messrs. A. Hall & Co. of Aberdeen, who built the *Stornoway*, the first typical clipper in the China tea trade, and notable for a run from Hong-Kong to the Downs in 102 days. A fine rigged model of a wooden built clipper ship, the *Stonehouse*, completed in 1866, is illustrated in fig. 3; the hull was made by Mr. Row in 1871 and the masting, rigging and sails added in the South Kensington Museum in 1906. The original was 209 ft. long, 36 ft. beam, and 21 ft. deep and a gross registered tonnage of 1153 tons; the model is built to a scale of $\frac{1}{4}$ in. to 1 foot, and is a very fine piece of work.

The fine example of ship modelling illustrated in fig. 4 portrays the *Sudbourne*, a full-rigged ship built of iron at Stockton-on-Tees in 1881, and now on exhibition at the Science Museum. Her registered tonnage was 1750 tons, length 265 ft., breadth 39 ft., and depth 24 ft. This model is also to a scale of $\frac{1}{4}$ in. to 1 ft. which allows of finely detailed work.

The last and largest of the "White Star" sailing clippers, the *California*, built and equipped at Belfast in 1890 by Harland & Wolff, had a length of 329 ft., breadth 45 ft. and gross register 3099 tons. The model shown in fig. 5 is to a

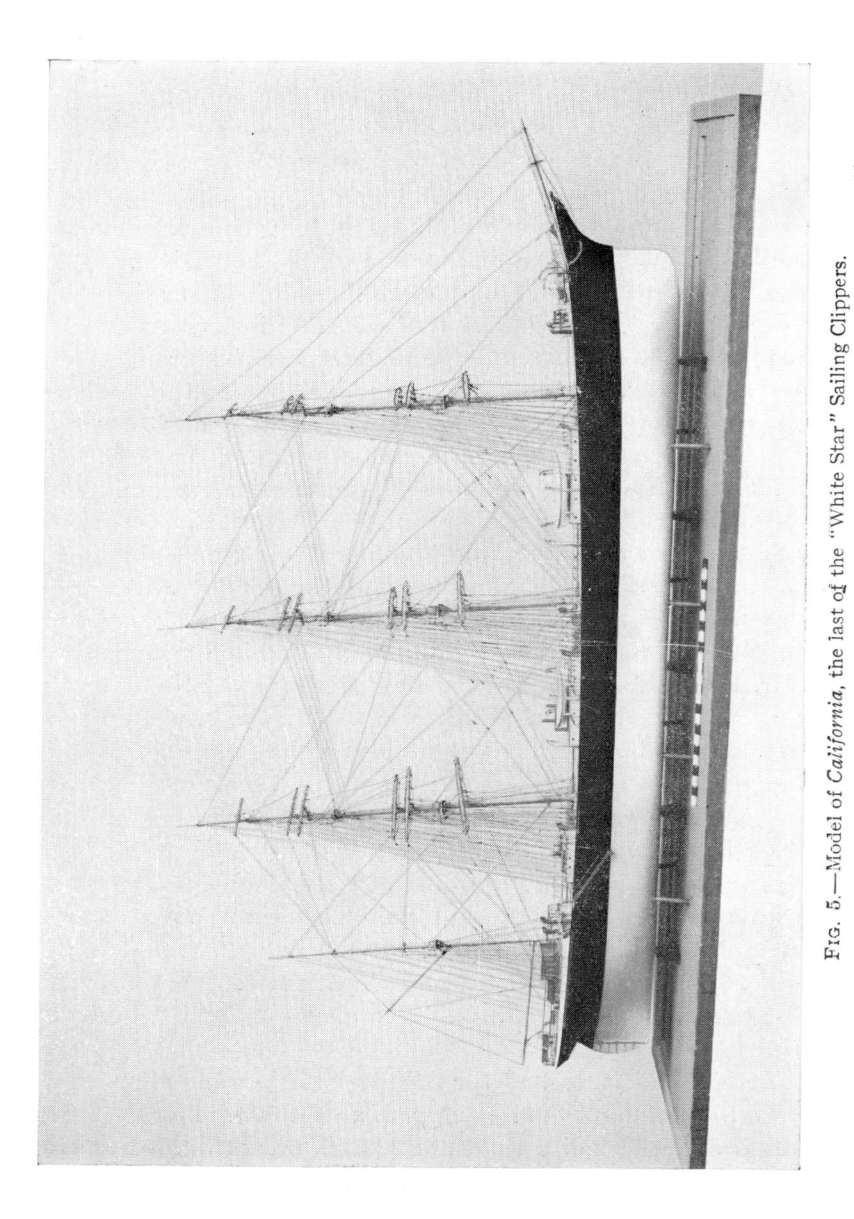

FIG. 5.—Model of *California*, the last of the "White Star" Sailing Clippers.

Fig. 6.—Model of Four-Masted Barque-rigged Clipper Ship *Pass of Melfort.*

scale of $\frac{1}{4}$ in. to 1 ft., and gives a fine impression of the ultimate development of the clipper ship.

The *Pass of Melfort* shown in fig. 6 is a model of another of the latest clippers, a four-masted barque-rigged ship built of steel at Glasgow in 1891 by the Fairfield Shipbuilding and Engineering Co. She is not so large as the *California*; her particulars are gross register 2346 tons, length 298 ft., breadth 44 ft., depth 24 ft. 6 ins.; her lower and topmasts are in one piece, and she has double topsail and topgallant yards and steam power is provided for the heavy work on the ship.

Future generations will look back upon our models of to-day hoping to learn from them something of the splendour, the folly and the joy of the clipper ship. Let us therefore, while there is yet time, leave them worthy memorials that will ultimately attain the preciousness of bygone things.

CHAPTER II.

BUILDING CLIPPER MODELS.

General Introduction to the Subject—Various Ways Briefly Indicated, with Notes on Technical Requirements and Skill—Tools and Materials needed are Few and Simple to Use—Outlined Diagrams of Three Typical Clippers.

BEFORE we actually commence to build a ship model, let us pause and ask what it is we want to do and why we want to do it. We shall probably do it because deep down within us is an inherited love of the sea and ships, because we find pleasure in their presence—or it may be that commercial instincts arise, and well deserved profits may follow the persistent demand from collectors and others for good ship models. Between the enthusiast on one side, and the commercially inspired constructor on the other, range those who desire a model for its sheer beauty—those who love ship modelling for its value as a recreative hobby, those who need a memento of the old days, and the historian or student who conceives that scrupulous accuracy is all important.

No matter for what reason a ship model is constructed it must have character, it must be made to live, to typify the actual ship, to express something of the virtues or the vices of the real thing. A good model is always an expression of the thing modelled, and, unlike most other modes of self-expression, should not give any clue to the personality of the maker. It must be the real ship, it must express the spirit of the ship and the sea!—in a word, when anyone looks at the model they should immediately think of a ship, should praise or blame the ship and not the model. The true test of a good model is its character and not the excellence of the workmanship. No matter how crude the work put into a model, it is still a good model, if when we are looking at it we say, what a fine old ship, and only then remember that we are looking at a model.

Perhaps as you read this you will think these sentiments are far fetched, the idle vapourings of a dreamer; not so my friend, put it to the test yourself! It will not cost you much in hard cash to pass the threshold and taste the first joys of ship modelling, a few pence will suffice, yet with nothing more elaborate than matches and a few odd bits of card we will conjure up together a memory of past ships and gallant seamen, and you, my friend, will find the hours pass lightly as the model grows beneath your eyes.

There are three great groups or types of ship models, firstly, the small waterline models, made with little bits of card, paper, pins, matches and other homely items, to represent a ship as seen far out at sea. The second group comprises scenic or sketch models, which strive to convey atmosphere and character only, and are usually accompanied by painted backgrounds and plaster waves. Thirdly, there are the exquisite exhibition or scale models in which every part is faithfully represented to proper proportion, and included in this class are sectional models exhibiting internal and other details of construction. There are other models, if they can be so designated, such as the fully rigged ship in a bottle, models made with sea shells or other weird and unsuitable materials, all more or less freaks despite the painstaking ingenuity of their constructors.

There is no basis of comparison between these classes. The waterline models are fascinating, make the greatest call on the imagination, detail is conspicuously absent, but the true feeling, proportion and character of the real ship are very apparent when the model is seen from the correct viewpoint, that is, on a line with the eyes.

In the second class the models are generally larger and show much more detail, but here again the art is to suggest by implication rather than to demonstrate by the actual profusion of detail.

The third category is in quite a different class and calls for very much technical skill and constructive ability. To make a really complete clipper ship model similar to the best work turned out by commercial firms is generally beyond the scope of the non-professional model maker, although with the practice of sufficient patience and common sense

FIG. 7.
Model of Clipper Ship built by H. H. Marsden, Esq.

it is open to anyone, of either sex, to ultimately complete a work in nowise inferior, as is demonstrated in fig. 7, by Mr. H. H. Marsden's fine model clipper.

The best plan for the novice is first to make a waterline model then a scenic model, and after thus gaining some technical ability, particularly the knack of handling the numerous small pieces, to undertake the more intricate work involved in the construction of a scale model such as the

Fig. 8.—*Loch Torrens* Finished.

Loch Torrens illustrated in the Frontispiece. As a guide to the determination of a suitable scale it may be pointed out that most exhibition models are made to a scale of $\frac{1}{4}$ in. equals 1 foot, in other words they are 1/48 full size. This enables complete detail to be shown but makes a bulky and expensive model. The smallest practical scale for a model with fairly complete detail is 1/12 inch equalling one foot, as adopted for the *Loch Torrens* (fig. 8), producing a model about 30 inches overall length. Waterline models can have scales ranging between 1/100 inch equaling one foot to, say, 1/30 inch equaling 1 foot, the models measuring about 2 inches and

FIG. 9.
Relative Scales Compared.

9 inches in overall length respectively; compare fig. 9 showing Nelson's *Victory* to a scale of 1/100 inch equaling 1 foot, with *Cutty Sark* to a scale of 1/30 inch equaling 1 foot.

Scenic models such as fig. 10 can be about 1/25 to 1/10 inch equalling 1 foot, and then require a case measuring roughly 30 inches to 6 feet in length respectively.

As regards tools and materials, the equipment will depend largely on the inclination of the builder, some can do wonders with a few common tools, others require a fully equipped workshop. Suffice it to say that no special tools are necessary for any of the models in the first two classes.

So far as technical ability is concerned it is safe to say that anyone with two hands can, by following the instructions in the next chapter, make a successful waterline model. Most people could make a scenic model; and practically all

FIG. 10.

Scenic Model of *Cutty Sark.*

who succeeded with both these models would find that when they want to they can make a scale model, as quite unconsciously they will have learnt the rudiments of many useful handicrafts, and can supplement that knowledge very readily by consulting some of the excellent technical manuals on the market.

Before going further, it may be helpful to mention a few of the technical names of the more important parts of a ship, names applied to most square-rigged clippers.

The outline diagram (fig. 11) represents a "ship" as understood by sailormen, a three-master with square sails on each mast. The barque shown in fig. 12 has square sails on the fore and main masts only, the mizen being rigged like a schooner. The names of the masts, sails and rigging are rather confusing to the novice, especially as there appears to be a veritable maze of ropes on a well-made model. Fortunately they are all named on a regular plan (with a few exceptions) and are comparatively universal in their application. At

FIG. 11.
Diagram of Full Rigged Ship.

FIG. 12.
Diagram of a Barque.

this stage we shall only be concerned with a few of these names as indicated on the diagram (fig. 13) by the letters.

Starting at the forward end or bows *A*, the first mast ***B*** is always called the foremast, next comes the mainmast ***C***, then the mizen mast ***D***. In a four-masted ship the fourth mast is termed a jigger-mast, and in the case of a five-masted ship the fifth mast is termed the after-jiggermast. All these masts usually consist of three parts—the lower, middle and upper parts, respectively called the lower mast, topmast and topgallant mast. In most ships the topgallant mast has a separate mast formed in one with it, although it is sometimes mounted independently and known as the royal mast, or royal pole. The various masts are distinguished by the general name prefixed to that of the parts of the mast. Thus the lower mast nearest to the bows is always the fore lower mast *E*, or more shortly, the foremast; the topmast on the fore becomes the fore topmast *F*, and so on. It is therefore, a simple matter to remember the proper names. The rule is first to name the position of the whole of the mast, for example, fore, main or mizen—then add the name of the part of the mast. For example—foremast *B*, main topgallant mast *G*, mizen topmast *H*, fore topmast *F*, and so on.

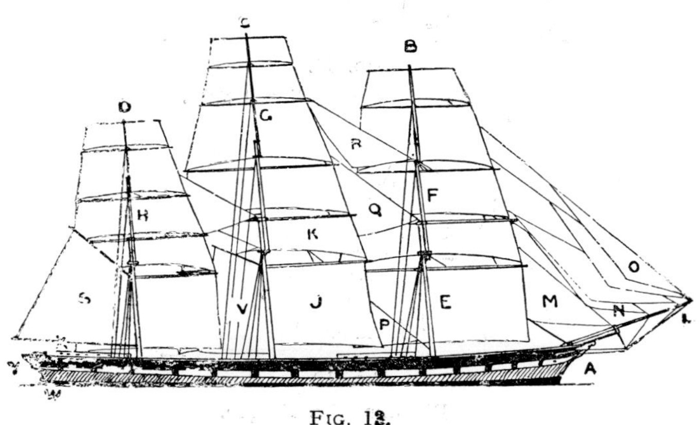

Fig. 12.
Names of Principal Parts of a Ship Model.

The square sails are named from the deck upwards, as follows—sail, or course, lower topsail, upper topsail, lower topgallant, upper topgallant, royal, skysail, moonraker. To these are prefixed the name of the mast, thus the lowest sail of the mainmast *J* is called the mainsail, or main course, then the main lower topsail *K*, and so on. The topsail and topgallant sails are not always divided but the two are combined into one sail called the topsail and topgallant sail, respectively. The headsails, mounted on stays between the foremast and the bowsprit *L*, are generally named after the stay that supports them, as follows—that next to the mast is the fore topmast staysail *M*, the next is the inner jib *N*, outer jib (if the jib is divided, as is often the case), and finally the flying jib *O* or foreroyal staysail. The outer jib is frequently called the fore topgallant staysail. The fore and aft sails between the masts are designated by the names of the stays supporting them, thus from the deck upwards, topmast staysail *P*, topgallant mast staysail *Q*, and royal staysail *R*, with the prefix of the name of the mast that the stay supports. The fore and aft sail on the mizen mast is called the spanker *S*, and a sail when mounted above it, as on a barque, is called the gaff topsail. The spars or yards are named after the sails, thus the yard that carries the main royal sail is known as the main royal yard, and so on. The masts are supported by strong ropes called stays and shrouds. Stays support a mast in a fore and aft direction and are named according to the part supported. Shrouds support a mast in a lateral direction, and are described by the name of the mast supported; thus the shrouds *V* which support the mainmast are known as the main shrouds. The part of a mast where an upper mast is parallel to a lower mast is called the doubling, and the parts which fasten them together are called tops on a lower mast, and crosstrees on upper masts. The fitting at the extreme top of any mast which holds any mast above it is called a cap. At the top of the entire mast is a finial known as the truck. The parts of the hull (for the purpose of model makers) are the bows or extreme front end part, the stern, or after part *W*, the waist, or middle part of the deck, often called amidships. Accommodation at the bows is known as the forecastle, that at the stern as the poop *X*. The overhanging part at the stern is called the counter *Y*, and its line of junction with the body of the hull as the knuckle.

CHAPTER III.

MAKING A WATERLINE MODEL.

A Thing Anyone can Make in a Few Evenings—Very Picturesque when done—Complete Details of the Aspects of the Work with Full Size Line Drawings of Each Part and Several Photographs of the Work Actually in Progress and a Photograph of the Finished Model.

The expression "waterline" model is generally applied to small models, which represent a ship when afloat and seen at a distance, consequently only that part of the hull which is visible above water is modelled; they rely for effect on what is suggested or inferred and not upon minute details, but must necessarily be accurate as regards general proportions and outline.

Every novice to ship modelling should commence by making one or more of these little models, to acquire a certain dexterity of manipulation, a sense of touch and a comprehension of proper proportion.

In the ordinary way, a waterline model of a clipper ship, such as *Cutty Sark*, fig. 14, can be made to a scale of 30 ft. to 1 inch by anyone in the course of a few evenings' work; all the operations can if desired be carried out on the dining table, there is no mess or bother and nothing in the way of tools except a pocket knife, a piece of sandpaper, and a tube of seccotine. The materials needed are an odd piece of soft straight grained wood about 3/8 ins. thick, such as can be had from almost any small wooden packing box or the like,

FIG. 14.
Waterline Model of *Cutty Sark.*

a sheet of thin cardboard, or in emergency, a postcard or two, a few long match sticks, a reel of black thread and a sheet of thin white paper, fig. 15, showing the entire collection.

FIG. 15.
Everything required for Making a Waterline Model.

One or two sheets of strawboard, and a packet of pins are very handy for holding pieces together while the seccotine is drying, and if working in a living room, it is just as well to have a piece of smooth wood on which to work, to avoid any accidental scratches on the polished surface of a table.

For the attempt let *Cutty Sark* be chosen as the prototype and modelled to a scale of 30 ft. to 1 in. or as nearly to that scale as may be feasible. The first part to make is the hull, which consists of a flat piece of wood 8 ins. long, $1\frac{1}{4}$ in. wide, 5/16 in. thick, and smooth on both faces. The outline of the deck, as shown in fig. 16, has now to be drawn on the upper surface, either by placing the wood beneath the diagram and marking it out with the aid of carbon paper, placed with its face against the wood, or by setting out the shape with a pair of compasses.

The latter operation is performed by drawing a centre line along the middle of the wood corresponding with the centre line on the diagram and drawing other lines at right angles to it, similarly spaced to those on the diagram (fig. 16) plate No. 6. The compasses or dividers are then adjusted to the distance along the first of these lines, measuring from the centre outwards to the curved line and this dimension transferred to the corresponding cross line on the wood, and marked on each side of the centre line. Treat each cross line or section in the same way, and draw a fair curve through these points. Cut the wood to this shape, with the pocket knife or a small fretsaw if the latter is available, and trim it up carefully to exact shape by long strokes with a piece of medium grade sandpaper. Then draw on the underside of this block the outline of the load waterplane shown in fig. 17, and with a pocket knife carve the hull sides to shape. The bows will be practically V-shaped in cross sections, but the stern as seen in fig. 18 is more undercut to represent the counter.

Take care to preserve the characteristic knuckle at the counter or underside of the stern, as shown in the profile view in fig. 18 and clearly seen in fig. 19, and make the whole quite smooth and true by sandpapering. The next pieces to prepare are the cardboard side pieces or bulwark strakes as shown in fig. 20. These as can be seen in fig. 21 have to be bent and fastened to the sides of the hull, to impart the sheer or curve to the hull and toprail, and to represent the bulwarks.

The shape for these cards, of which two are required, is given in fig. 20 and they should be cut from 2 or 3-ply Bristol board, or other thin smooth card. Bend them around the hull and fix them temporarily with pins as seen in fig. 21, and take care that they fit closely to the hull from the bows to the stern, but they do not fit beneath the knuckle or turn of the counter at the stern.

FIG. 19.
Shaping the Stern.

Leave them in this position and disregard the surplus at this stage, meanwhile proceed to cut out the pieces of card to represent the deck erections. These are all shown in fig. 22 to the same proportion as the hull diagrams and have only to be cut to the shapes given. The part *A* is for the poop deck and should be about 1/8 inch thick or rather less; part *C* is the midship house and needs two pieces of thick card both the same shape and seccotined together. The part *B* is for the hatches, and should be quite thin; two separate pieces are needed, *D* is the forecastle and should be as thick as *A*, and the same thickness can be used for the steering gear casing *E*, the after deckhouse *F*, and the skylight *G*, placed on top of the deckhouse *F* towards its fore end, and both of them are then placed on the forward part of the poop. The skylight *H* fits on the after end of the midship deckhouse *C*, while the hatches come on the centre line between the forecastle and foremast, and between the main and mizen masts respectively as is clear from fig. 21.

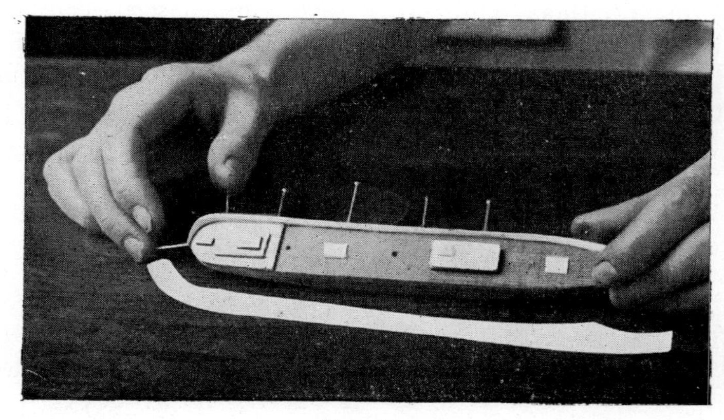

Fig. 21.
Fixing Bulwark Strakes to Hull.

Fix these pieces in place with seccotine and then cut four pieces of card as at *J* (fig. 22) and fasten them together in pairs. When the adhesive is dry they are sandpapered to the familiar shape of a ship's lifeboat, and later on are fixed to boat skids *K*, made from bent pins with the heads cut off, and the ends pressed into the hull and with the skid part resting on the top of the midship deckhouse, these pieces being shown in fig. 14.

Now run a pencil around inside the bulwark cards, and remove them from the hull block, and carefully cut away any surplus card, but leave a good 1/8 inch above the marked lines. Permanently refix these cards with seccotine, and force them into close contact with the hull by repinning as before. Take care to make a perfect joint at the centre of the counter, by fixing both the cards so that one overlaps the other, then before the adhesive sets make one clean cut with a very sharp knife through both the cards, remove the surplus, and hold the two ends in contact with pins.

When the seccotine is quite hard—but not before—the surplus card is cut away, and the upper edge made into a perfect curve by sandpapering it until there is only about 1/8 inch or rather less of the card standing above the upper surface of the hull block to represent the bulwarks. A brisk rub with very fine sandpaper over the whole exterior of the card will speedily remove all pin marks, and produce a nicely curved hull, with a perfectly smooth surface.

FIG. 24.
Tapering the Spars.

The masts and spars are made from thick round match-sticks or the like, Bryant & May's "Club" matches are splendid for the purpose and are first ignited and then cut to correct lengths as given in fig. 23, after which they are tapered and reduced in diameter in the manner pictured in fig. 24.

A block of wood with a shallow groove in one edge is laid on the table, and about half the length of the match rested in the groove. The outer end of the match is held between the thumb and first finger of the left hand, and slowly rotated, while briskly filing away the unwanted wood with a strip of medium (No. 1) sandpaper wrapped around the small flat file. This speedily reduces the diameter and tapers the match; those for the masts should taper gradually along the whole length, whereas for the yards the match has to be tapered from the centre towards each end.

The next operation is to make the "tops," the triangular shaped pieces shown at *L* in fig. 22, by marking the outline on a piece of card, piercing a hole for the lower mast and afterwards cutting the card to shape. This done, slip the tops on to the masts and secure them with seccotine. Next stick the topmasts in front of the lower masts with the bottom end or foot resting on the "top."

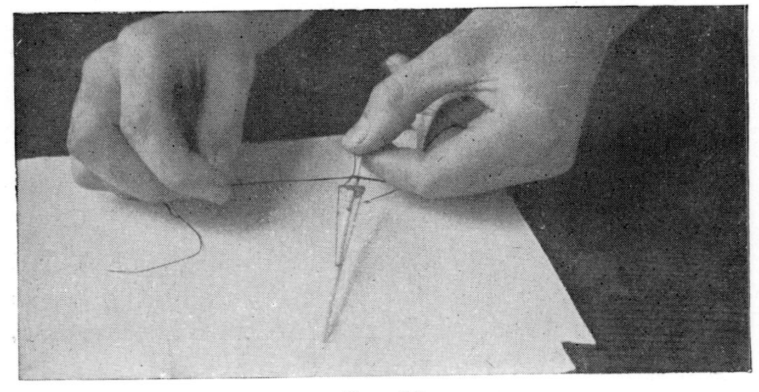

FIG. 25.
Fixing Topmast Shrouds.

As soon as the adhesive is dry, add the topgallant masts, fixing these in front of the topmasts as before, and allow the adhesive to set. Some simple rigging operations pictured in fig. 25, have now to be carried out, with ordinary black cotton to represent the topmast shrouds. Commence by cutting off a suitable length of cotton, say about 18 ins., and double it in the middle like a flattened *U*, and place the bight or bent part over the top of the topmast, and tie it there. Then hold the mast between the finger and thumb of the left hand, and with the right hand draw the two ends of cotton downwards and over the sides of the "top." Hold one of the cottons with the left hand, and with the right twist the other cotton around the mast a little below the top, and when so doing catch up the other cotton and thus grip it against the mast. Turn the two pieces of cotton once round the mast and tie them together as shown in fig. 25 and cut off the surplus ends.

Treat each mast in the same way, and then proceed to fix the lower shrouds, which consist of three pieces of cotton, tied in the middle to the lower mast immediately below the tops. To prevent any of these cottons slipping or becoming unfastened just put a tiny trace of adhesive on the knots and leave them to set hard. The next operation is to make the sails by cutting them to shape from any thin white or light buff coloured paper.

The proper sizes and shapes are given in fig. 26, but in some cases more than one sail has to be cut to the same pattern. Each sail is indicated by a letter and the following is a complete list of them, with the names of the sails.

No.			No.		
1	*A*	Mizen topgallant sail	1	*N*	Fore topgallant staysail
2	*B*	Mizen royal and main skysail	1	*O*	Main royal staysail
1	*C*	Fore royal	1	*P*	Fore topgallant staysail
1	*D*	Main royal	1	*Q*	Main topgallant staysail
2	*E*	Fore and main topgallant	1	*R*	Fore topmast staysail
1	*F*	Mizen upper topsail	1	*S*	Main staysail
1	*G*	Mizen lower topsail	1	*T*	Jib
2	*H*	Fore and main upper topsails	1	*U*	Mizen topgallant staysail
1	*J*	Mizen course	1	*V*	Mizen topmast staysail
2	*K*	Fore and main lower topsail	1	*W*	Spenser.
1	*L*	Spanker			
2	*M*	Fore and main course			

The square sails are mostly shown with little tabs at the clews or lower corners which are provided as a means of attaching the sail to the yard below it, but the spanker and spenser are shown with narrow strips for a similar purpose. All the square sails have now to be fixed to their respective yards by gumming the upper edge of the sail and attaching it neatly to the yard. Prepare the spanker and spenser in the same way, noting that the gaff or upper spar only is attached in this way, the clew of the spanker has a tab for fixing it to the boom (the lower spar), but the spenser has a short length of cotton stuck on to its clew. Both of these sails have tabs for attaching them to their masts.

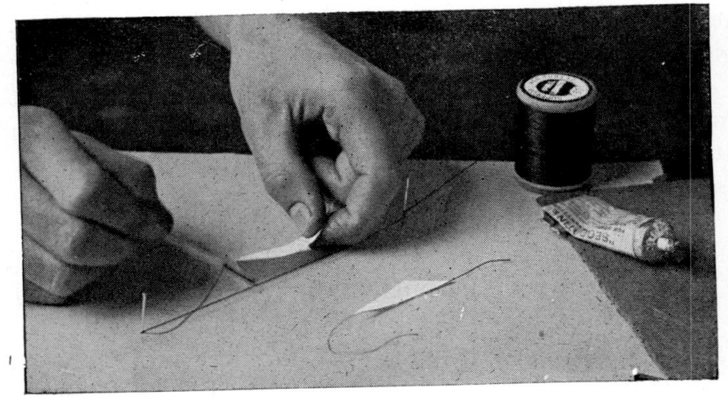

FIG. 27.
Fixing Head Sails to Cotton.

Prepare the headsails and staysails by gumming a long cotton to their longest edge, doing this as shown in fig. 27 by stretching the cotton tightly between two pins, applying the gum to the cotton and immediately pressing the sail into its place. After these are dry, gum a short length of cotton to the free corner of each sail to represent the "sheet."

The next operation is to assemble all the sails and spars for one mast, and to stick the tabs of the sails to the yards below them, taking care to keep all the yards parallel while doing so. Then lay the whole set flat on a piece of card and hold the yards in position by pins, as shown in fig. 28, and then put a touch of adhesive in the centre of each yard. Lay the mast in place and press it firmly into contact, and maintain it in position by a slip of wood, which presses on the mast and is held down by a pin driven through it as shown in the illustration.

FIG. 28.
Assembling the Spars and Sails.

Deal with all three masts in the same way, and while they are drying assemble the bowsprit and jibboom and fasten it in place at the bows.

Next make holes in the hull for the masts, and commence to set them up by fixing the foremast, fastening it as usual with adhesive. Then fix the headsails by twisting the lower end of the cotton around the bowsprit and fixing the upper end to the mast, with a simple knot, drawing the cotton taut but not straining the mast forwards.

Then fix the shrouds by simply sticking the lower ends of the three cottons to the upper outer edge of the hull, as shown in fig. 29, where the main shrouds are being fixed. The cottons already tied to the masts are of course used for this purpose, and three parts come on one side of the hull and the other three on the opposite side.

Fix the main and mizen masts in the same way, then add

the spanker and the spenser, and fix the staysails, the latter in the same manner as the headsails. The spanker and the spenser are both gummed directly to their masts, and then supported by little pieces of thin cotton gummed to the gaff and to the mast as shown on the photo of the finished model. The fore, main and mizen sheets are fixed in a similar manner, the sails being drawn backwards to give them a natural bulgeous appearance. It now only remains to paint the hull black, and add a couple of thin white lines, as shown in fig. 14, and to paint the decks a pale straw colour, the deck

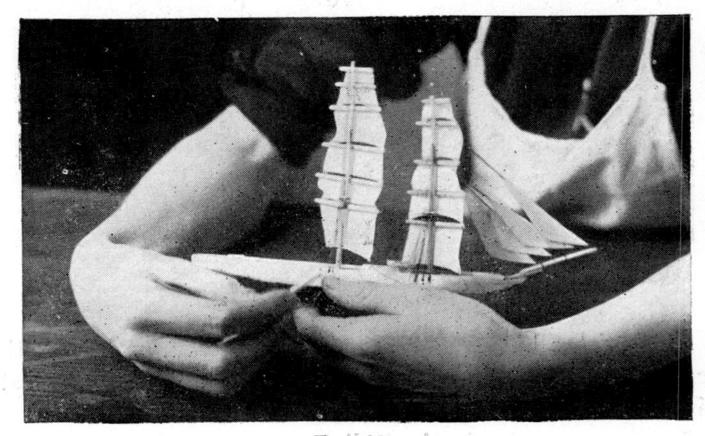

Fig. 29.
Securing Main Shrouds.

erections white, with the windows represented by little black dots. A little ornamentation in white at the bows and the stern will improve the appearance considerably. Any ordinary water colour paints will answer very well for this work especially if the lighter colours are well mixed with a good bodying of "Chinese" or "Process" white. The tops and caps can be picked out in black or any dark colour.

The general appearance of the model will be improved if the sails be pinched a little to make them curl and acquire a natural curved form suggesting they are full of wind and driving the ship at a good speed.

CHAPTER IV.

MAKING A SCENIC MODEL.

SCENIC MODELS REPRESENT THE SHIP UNDER SAIL AS IF AT SEA AND ARE LARGELY MADE FROM CARDBOARD AND OTHER SIMPLE MATERIALS—THE MODEL DESCRIBED IS LARGER THAN THE FOREGOING AND EXHIBITS DETAIL—THE WORK IS VERY SIMPLE BUT REMARKABLY EFFECTIVE—EVERY PROCESS DESCRIBED STEP BY STEP WITH ACTION PHOTOGRAPHS SHOWING STAGES IN THE WORK AND A PHOTOGRAPH OF THE FINISHED MODEL.

A SCENIC model is practically a picture in relief. As a rule it is housed in a glass case of some kind, usually with a hand-painted background, and the sea represented with plaster of Paris.

Scenic models are by no means to be despised, they have for many people a very real interest, and have a fascination peculiarly their own. Their purpose is in general to depict some characteristic action or phase of sea life, in contra-distinction to the mere reproduction of a particular vessel. For example, a ship may be represented as running before the gale in a wild sea, or perhaps weighing anchor and setting sail at dawn. Or it may be that a harbour and a lighthouse play a part in the story and are suitably depicted in the model. Another episode for a scenic model is a shipwreck with a rescue by the lifeboat.

Other aspects of scenic ship modelling may exhibit such features as a dredger at work in a harbour showing the boat and apparatus above and below water by depicting the surface of the water by a sheet of glass, or in other appropriate manner. Indeed, there are very many possibilities in scenic modelling, not the least being the introduction of clockwork or other motive power to actuate the ship, to make the waves sufficiently tempestuous, and so forth. This phase of the subject is however outside the scope of the present book, as it is more properly the sphere of the mechanician than that of the ship modeller.

When contemplating the construction of any scenic model, the first practical item to decide is the general overall size of the containing case. This may not sound right, but as an actual fact it is the available space for the display of the model that settles the dimensions of the case, and this must of necessity limit the scale or size of the ship model to be enclosed therein. The next point is to determine the most appropriate ship model size in relation to the case, bearing in mind the character of the ship, the scene portrayed and so forth. An example or two may help to make the matter clearer. Consider first a ship driving under a gale in heavy weather; here the background will be mostly dull grey in colour, indeterminate in form, suggesting driving spray and hurrying clouds with squalls of rain. The sea will be represented by few but great rolling waves, consequently there will be no need to suggest any considerable visible distances and therefore the ship model may occupy something of the order of, say, half the total available length. Had it been desired to depict a ship dropping the pilot as she clears the harbour bar on a quiet evening, and to show a distant range of cliffs, the curve of a great bay, with perhaps a suggestion of a quay in the foreground, then it would be necessary to greatly reduce the size of the ship relative to the case, and to model it to a smaller scale than the objects nearer to the eye. In other words, the scales of the notable features must be perspective, those things farthest away being to a smaller scale corresponding with the implied distances. Only in this way, coupled with correctly drawn perspective on the background, is it possible to impart the needful sense of space and distance.

The correct lighting of the whole scene is a matter of importance, as if the ship model throws a shadow on the back scene all impressions of distance are destroyed. Problems of this nature are far more acute in models intended for public exhibition or display purposes than they are when the model is intended for home adornment. Indeed, the subject is only mentioned here to indicate some of the points that will have to be dealt with by those who decide

Fig. 30.
Scenic Model in Case Complete.

to develop their work along these lines. Natural lighting, or illumination from outside the case, is usually most successful when the top of the case is glazed and strongly lighted from above and slightly in front of the case and general lighting provided by direct front lighting. Many charming effects are possible by electric lights concealed within the case, varying colours, changes of intensity and numerous theatrical and dramatic effects are then realisable.

An example of a scenic model chosen to demonstrate an

easy and successful method of construction is shown in fig. 30 and represents an early clipper ship driving before a gale under reduced canvas. The work involved in making it can be divided into three sections, firstly, the model of the clipper ship; secondly, the base, which includes the modelling of the waves; and thirdly, the background and enclosing case. The constructional details of the last item are fully dealt with in Chapter XV. to which reference should be made for additional information; suffice it to say here, that it consists of a simple proscenium or front frame with a clear glass window. The back is more or less semi-circular in plan, and there is in addition a similarly shaped baseboard, readily removable, through the rear aperture. The upper part of the case is glazed to admit top light, but if it is desired to add interior electric lights, sufficient space has been allowed behind the proscenium for the normal size electric bulbs. The only parts of this structure which concern the subject matter of this chapter are the removable baseboard, and a rectangular strip of good grade white drawing paper of a size to entirely cover the curved back of the case. It should be appreciated that a curved background is preferable because there are no awkward corners to deal with when the sides and back are combined into one whole strip.

Work is best commenced on the model of the clipper ship, and this being small can be constructed largely from cardboard. The hull is made on the cellular principle and is composed of three pieces of card:—One vertical central piece, one lower piece cut to the shape of the load water line, and one piece to the shape of the deck. These may have the same shapes as the profile, deck and water lines given in the previous chapter (figs. 16, 17, 18) or to suit the lines of the intended model. These cards should be cut to shape and their edges smoothed with sandpaper as shown in fig. 31, and note that the deck card has slots cut into it to allow the projecting parts of the central or profile card to pass through and is tried in place to ascertain if it is correct. The central member is then stuck with seccotine or other adhesive vertically on the centre line of the lower card and then a series of cross pieces of card have to be cut to fit in each side of the central card, and stuck into place as shown in fig. 32. The height of these pieces is to be equal to that of the profile card, except at bow and stern, where the height has to be such that the card will fill the space between the top of the lower member and the underside of the deck card. The widths of the cross pieces are determined by the curvature of the lower and deck cards, and terminate at their junction;

FIG. 31.
Smoothing Edge of Deck with Sandpaper.

thus the width of a cross piece on its lower edge is equal to the corresponding width on the lower (L.W.L.) card, and the width on the upper edge is equal to that of the deck card; hence on many of these cross pieces the end will have a definite slope or inclination. The number and spacing of the cross pieces is not critical, but on the average the cross pieces should be about $\frac{1}{2}$ inch apart at bow and stern, and rather wider apart amidships.

Assemble all these pieces while the lower card is held flat with drawing pins on a piece of smooth wood, as pictured in fig. 32 where pins are clearly shown supporting the various pieces while the adhesive is setting. When the adhesive has thoroughly dried and hardened, the drawing pins are removed and the upper edges of all the cross pieces of card are made level and true by careful sandpapering and the deck card is then fixed to their tops with adhesive; after it has set the ends of the cross pieces are smoothed with sandpaper

FIG. 32.
Assembling parts of the Hull.

and the side strips of 2-ply card cut to shape and fastened in position as shown in fig. 33. The exact shape for this card is preferably determined by making a paper pattern,

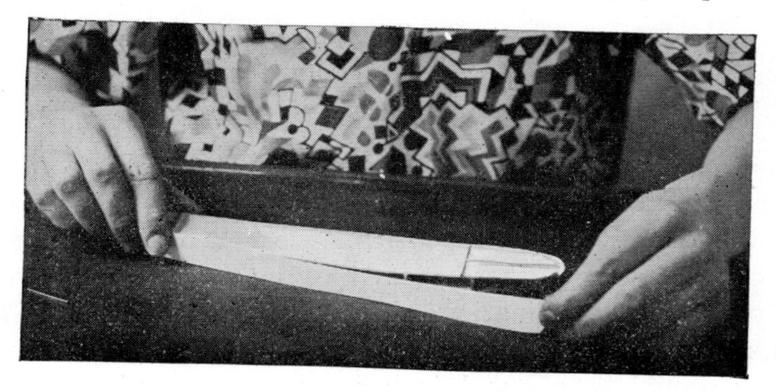

FIG. 33.
Fixing the Side Strip.

but will in any case take more or less the form shown in fig. 20, Chapter III. The poop and forecastle decks are added in a similar way to the waterline model, but as shown in fig. 33 cross pieces of card must be attached to the deck to form the bulkheads, and the deck pieces afterwards added as shown in fig. 34 and the hull completed by the addition of a

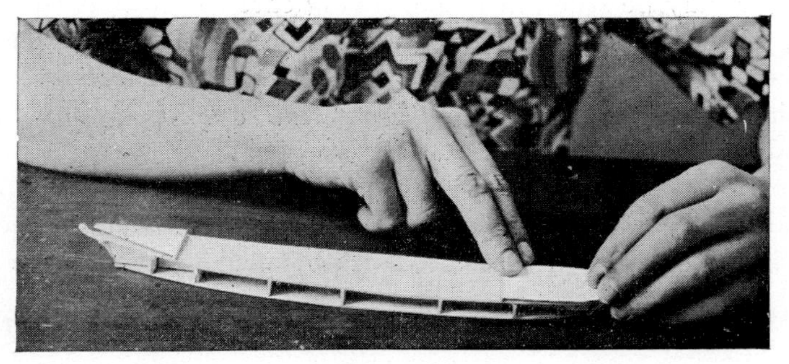

FIG. 34.
Fixing the Poop Deck.

little figurehead, after cleaning up all edges with very fine sandpaper.

Deck houses and other erections are then cut to shape

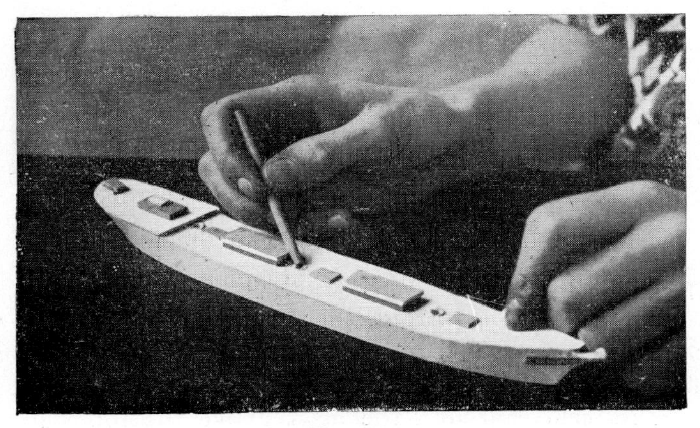

FIG. 35.
Hull showing Deck Erections.

from card or thin wood in a similar manner to the waterline model, and fastened to the deck with seccotine, the hull appearing as in fig. 35 at this stage. The holes for the masts are drilled with the aid of a hand-drill, and pieces of thin round wood inserted therein to represent the lower masts. These may be stuck in place, taking care to see that they are all in line, and correctly "raked" or inclined towards the stern. Now prepare the remainder of the masts and spars using long match sticks or thin round wood such as can be had from dealers in fretwork supplies. These are to be tapered by sandpapering as described in the previous chapter, and their sizes should be suitably proportioned or be in accordance with the selected prototype. Next prepare the

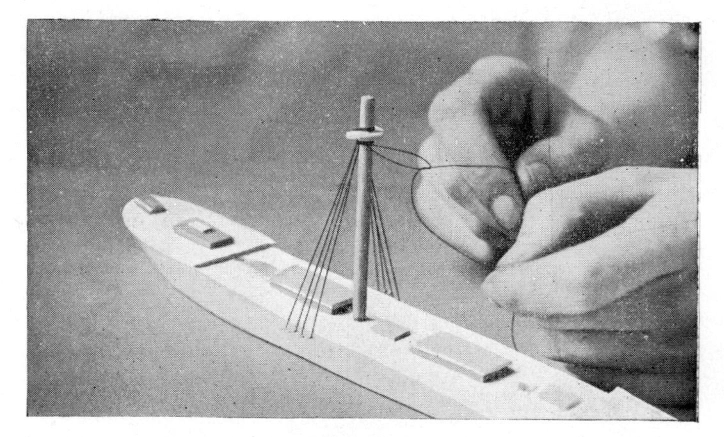

Fig. 36.
Fixing the Main Shrouds.

"tops" by cutting them from stout card after the holes for the masts have been pierced, then attach them to the lower masts with a trace of seccotine and fix the shrouds as shown in fig. 36. These are made from a single length of cotton tied in its centre around the mast above the top, and the ends taken down and under the foremost of a row of four pins temporarily driven into the hull on each side. Pass the cottons under the next pins and then up and over the top, cross them around the mast and then down under the remaining pins and up again to the top, again crossed and then taken to the underside of the top and turned twice around the shrouds and fastened by knotting the ends as in fig. 36 which draws the shrouds taut. Fasten the shrouds to the hull sides with seccotine, and when dry remove the pins.

Assemble the topmasts and topgallant masts by sticking them at the "doubling" or part where the two overlap and represent the caps by a narrow strip of paper or thin card glued in position. The cross trees and spreaders are represented by thin strips of card and pins respectively, as shown in fig. 37, and when finished can be painted with egg-shell

Fig. 37.
Detail of Topmast and Crosstrees.

black, and will then look quite realistic for a model of this class. These masts are then assembled in their proper places on the lower masts in a similar way and the topmast shrouds and backstays fitted. The bowsprit and jibboom are then fitted and the stays represented by cotton or thread, secured in place with seccotine as described in the previous chapter. The shrouds need not have ratlines or any smaller details, and if the standing rigging is arranged as shown in several of the photos, and particularly in fig. 38, will look very effective. The next proceeding consists of attaching the spars to the masts which can be done with a fine pin driven through the spar, and further secured with a spot of adhesive. Remember to set the yards horizontally, but diagonally, across the ship, in accordance with the general scheme, so that when completed the sails will come in the proper positions relative to the wind and sea. Note that for subjects such as this the upper sails, skysails and royals would normally be furled and the yards lowered, consequently they should be so represented on the model. The next proceeding after fixing the yards is to add the various lifts,

FIG. 38.
The Standing Rigging.

or those ropes reaching from the ends of the yards to an elevated position on the mast. The disposition of the various ropes to be included on the model are clearly shown in the photographic reproductions and should make the rigging a comparatively simple matter even for the uninitiated.

The sails next call for attention, and are best made from thin flexible paper cut to shape in a similar way to those for the waterline model, and subsequently attached to the spars by sticking the upper edge or "head" of the sail to the yard with a little gum or other adhesive. The lower corners or clews are similarly fixed to the lower yards. It is, however, necessary to shape the sails so that they will bulge or belly out correctly and appear as if they really were filled with wind. This modelling can be done by damping the paper and

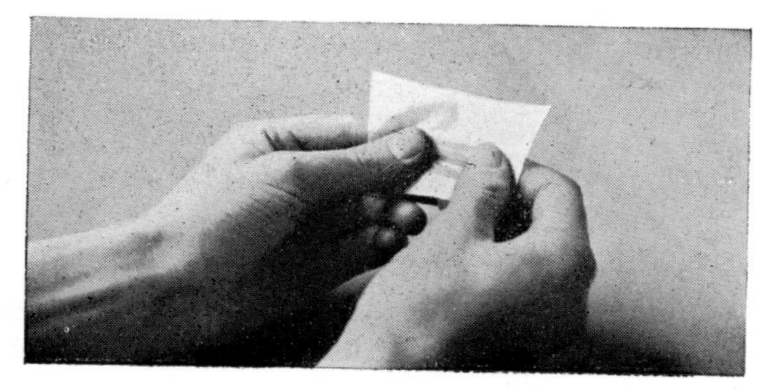

FIG. 39.
Stretching the Middle ot the Sail.

FIG. 40.
Curving the Fore Topgallant Stay.

carefully stretching and working it between the fingers and thumb as in fig. 39 until it bulges, and then working a little starch water into the sail by dipping the fingers into the liquid and kneading or working it into the paper. As soon as the sails are comparatively dry they can be attached to their yards and any additional modelling then effected. The head-sails and the courses or lower sails on yards will need different treatment as regards their rigging to that followed on the waterline models, as if cottons are used for the "sheets" the sail will not keep in place, consequently it is preferable to make the main sheets and the like from very thin wire such as bouquet or floral wire, carefully bent to shape, and attached to the foot of the sail along the whole of its length and then bent to a correct curvature. The headsails are similarly treated and the wire curved while in place as shown in fig. 40 to give the desired sense of motion. The furled sails are easily represented by suitably rolled pieces of paper, and then the braces and other details added and the model painted in any appropriate or desired colours.

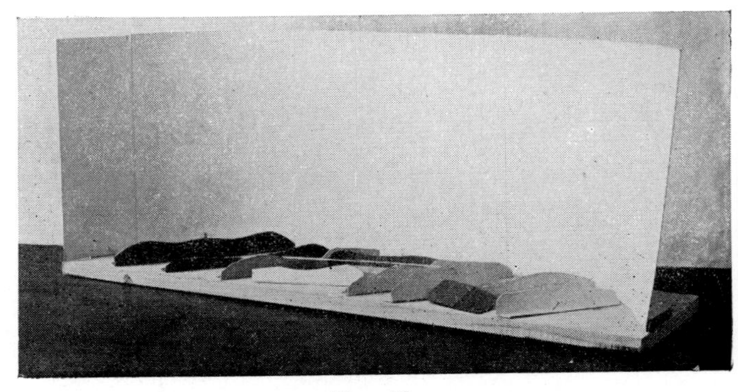

FIG. 41.
Baseboard prepared with Contoured Card.

Now comes the modelling of the waves, which can be effected in several ways. They could be modelled in ordinary modelling clay, or roughly formed in solid plaster of Paris and then carved to shape, but the most successful method is first of all to fasten odd pieces of wood or card to the base-board as in fig. 41, shaped and disposed to represent the tops of the waves. Next prepare several pieces of butter muslin,

Fig. 42.

Impregnating the Muslin with Plaster of Paris.

Fig. 43.

Placing the Muslin on the Base.

or some similar material, each of a size sufficient to entirely cover the area of the baseboard. This muslin is impregnated with superfine plaster of Paris by laying the muslin on a sheet of paper and working the plaster into the apertures with the fingers as shown in fig. 42, the pieces are then rolled up lightly and laid aside until required. Wet the edges of the contoured cards and then immerse the prepared muslin in warm water, lightly wring it out like a dishcloth, unfold it and spread it over the base as in fig. 43, allowing it to sag into hollows between the wave crests. Add sufficient pieces in a similar way until a firm surface results, which usually calls for about four thicknesses. At each stage in these

Fig. 44.
Modelling the Waves.

proceedings, place the ship model in position and press it down sufficiently to form a flat place for it to ultimately rest upon. Then before the plaster has set hard, mix up some more of the plaster to form a thick paste and brush it over the surface, and further model the waves as in fig. 44 with the aid of a simple spoon-ended wooden modelling tool. Represent the waves by bold, long, sweeping strokes, and afterwards pay attention to surface markings. This part of the work calls for some amount of artistic feeling, but the operations themselves are quite simple and straightforward. When the base has thoroughly dried, any surplus material around the edges is trimmed off with a sharp knife and the base inserted into the casing. The back scene is then put into position and the waves as indicated by the curved edges of the base are lightly marked on the back scene with a very soft pencil. The back scene is then removed and painted with water colours in as realistic a manner as possible, taking care to blend the modelled waves on the base into others represented by paintwork on the back scene. No specific instructions can be given for this sort of work, it is so much a matter of personal feeling and ability. The paper should in any case be well damped before applying the colours and a good even wash of blue or gray worked over the sky and a deeper and more green colour washed across the lower part. Clouds and waves are then worked in with as much realism as possible, some good effects being obtained by wiping off any excess of colour with a clean rag—a method that is usually highly successful in the reproduction of cloud forms. When this back scene is dry it is inserted in place and secured to the back of the case with a few touches of seccotine. The waves will have to be painted with poster colours or with oil colours, and the colours and treatment should blend into the back scene, the strength of the colour and the amount of detail shown being greatest in the foreground to aid in the illusion of distance. When the waves are thus far completed, stick the ship model in place and make up any slight deficiencies around it with plastic wood, or plaster, and colour it to suit. The effect of breaking seas is attained either with bold blobs of white paint, or by sticking cotton wool to the wave crests, and when dry carefully combing or teasing it to a light and feathery edge. A good photograph or painting is a great help in the modelling as it assists in attaining that atmosphere and character so necessary in a model of this class.

CHAPTER V.

MODELLING THE HULL.

THIS CHAPTER DEALS EXHAUSTIVELY WITH ALL ASPECTS OF MAKING CLIPPER HULLS FROM THE SOLID AND ALSO BY THE COMPOSITE METHOD—ILLUSTRATED WITH LINE DIAGRAMS AND PHOTOGRAPHS.

THE hull of any model is a very important part, and it is essential that it be correctly formed. The shape will have been determined by the designer, and that shape recorded in the form of a drawing prepared in the special way practised by naval architects. These drawings are usually called the lines and consist of a series of sections taken at regular or predetermined positions.

The preparation of a set of hull lines such as those in plate No. 2 either for a model or a real ship is a matter for considerable technical knowledge and skill, coupled with lengthy practical experience. The whole performance speed and stability of the ship depend in no small measure upon the ability of the designer, and the skill with which he meets a variety of conflicting requirements and conditions. Fortunately we are not now concerned with problems of design, but have merely to so fashion our material that the external shape will correctly interpret the lines themselves.

The lines are based upon a horizontal plane known as the Load Water Line and marked L.W.L. on most drawings. This represents the plane of flotation, or the surface of the water wherein the hull is floating when normally loaded. Other horizontal planes are drawn parallel to L.W.L. both above and below it and represent horizontal sections through the hull, and appear as horizontal lines in the elevation or sheer plan of the hull, and as curved lines on the half breadth plan the shapes of the latter representing the outer surfaces of the hull at that position. Other sections are taken across and at right angles to the waterplanes and appear as straight lines on the sheer and half breadth plans, but as curved lines on the body plan.

Actually the points of intersection of the curves in the body plan with the horizontal waterplanes appear as corresponding widths or heights, as the case may be, on the sheer and half breadth plans. It is usual on ship drawings only to depict one half of the hull, as the opposite halves are naturally alike. The hull is therefore drawn as if divided into two along the vertical centre line, and for convenience the sections from the bow to amidships are drawn on one side of the centre line on the body plan, and the sections from amidships towards the stern on the other side. All the sections and waterplanes are correspondingly lettered or numbered for easy identification.

In addition, there are other section lines sometimes shown on hull drawings but they do not directly concern the making of a model hull. In passing it may be well to mention that vertical planes parallel to the centre line are known as buttock lines and appear as curves in the sheer plan and as straight lines on the body and half breadth plans. Radial lines called diagonals are frequently shown, and depict the curvature of the skin of the hull along a plane inclined at some angle to the L.W.L. They are very useful to the designer, but may be neglected by the builder of a model.

As the foregoing is almost universal it is well to grasp the meaning and inter-connection of these lines, and to realise that in making a model hull everything is worked from the horizontal plane known as the L.W.L.

No matter what sort of hull is to be made it is essential to know the shape of various sections conveniently distributed along the hull and at right angles to its centre line, such sectional forms being given in the body plan.

The photographs of a specially prepared model yacht hull may assist in a comprehension of the inter-relationship

FIG. 45.
Sectioned Model of a Yacht Hull to show the Lines.

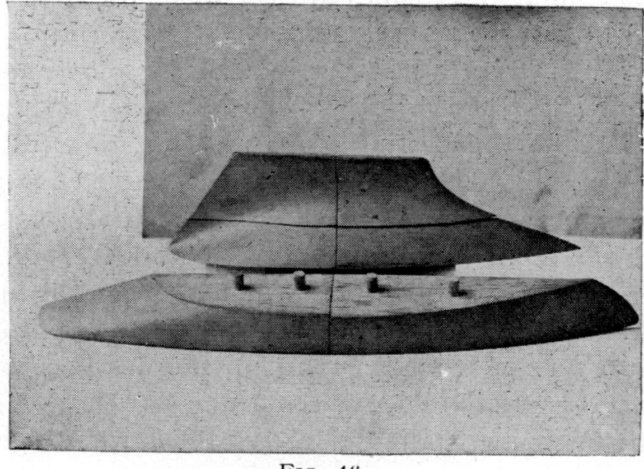

FIG. 46.
The Hull severed to show the Waterplane.

of these lines, and although the yacht hull differs considerably to a clipper hull the principles are the same in each case.

In fig. 45 the hull is shown as if cut asunder across the

centre and the section thus revealed exhibits the midship section as it would be drawn on the body plan. In the next illustration (fig. 46) the hull is shown as if severed along the L.W.L. and a second cut made parallel to it, to represent a waterplane. Note how these lines appear in the body plan as straight lines, but as curves in the half breadth plan. The relationship of these lines is further elucidated in fig. 47 showing the parts assembled, but leaving the joints distinctly visible. These joints in this model represent the L.W.L., and a horizontal waterplane parallel to it, corresponding

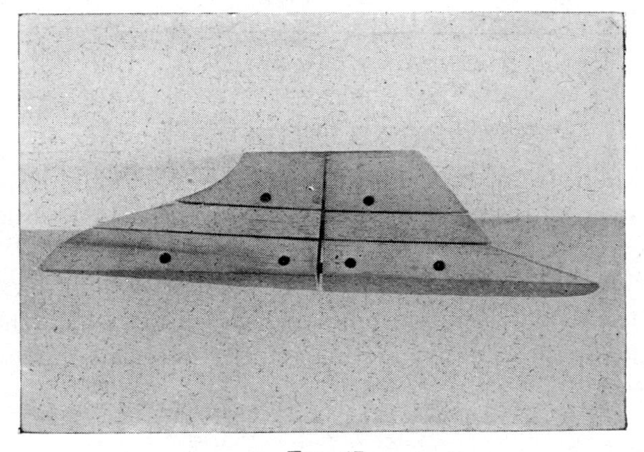

Fig. 47.
Sectional Hull Assembled.

with L.W.L. and W. in the diagram, fig. 48, which is a simplified drawing of the model yacht hull, the cut across the hull being represented by the cross section line *M S* on the sheer and half breadth plans, and by the curve on the body plan. The dowel pins and holes visible in the photographs are only needed for this demonstration model and are not reproduced on an actual hull.

When drawings are not available, it is necessary to prepare them specially, utilising all available data, and some hints on this matter will be found in Chapter XVI., but a complete dissertation on the subject is outside the scope of this book, nor would it serve any useful purpose as a number of drawings are included to guide the amateur ship modeller, and others

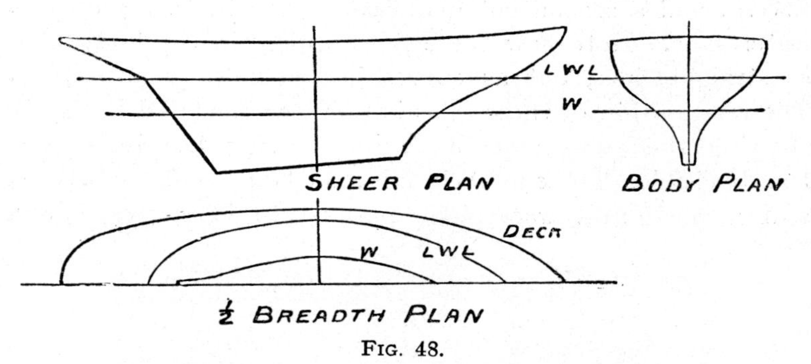

FIG. 48.
Simplified Drawing of Hull shown in Fig. 47.

can be had from Bassett-Lowke Ltd., Northampton, who specialise in the supply of designs and components for ship models.

Having become possessed of a set of lines suitable for a model, the next consideration is the system on which the hull is to be made. Many methods and materials have been

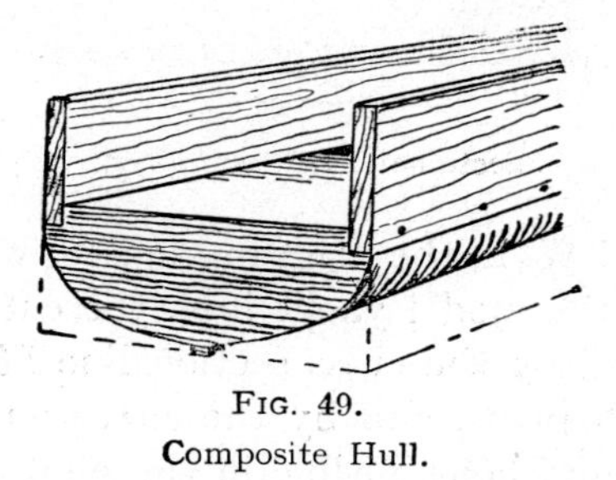

FIG. 49.
Composite Hull.

advocated from time to time. One way is to carve the hull from a solid block of wood, another plan is to use a thick piece of wood for the lower part of the hull, and to set vertical planks upon it, curved to the shape of the deck, a method known as the composite and illustrated in fig. 49 in diagrammatic form, but it is not often used for clipper models. Many excellent old ship models have been built in true nautical style with ribs and separate planks, a system known as the rib and plank, and dealt with in detail in Chapter VI.

Hulls are frequently made by cutting a series of planks to the shapes of the waterplanes, and then fastening them one on top of another, known as the bread and butter system and dealt with in detail in Chapter VIII., under the heading of making the hull for the *Loch Torrens*, or to exhibit the form

FIG. 50.
Hull of the *Fiery Cross*.

of the waterlines as in the case of the *Fiery Cross* shown in fig. 50, a China tea clipper built in 1860.

Still another method is to fashion a number of planks to the shape of the buttock lines and to fasten them together in a vertical position, but this is only a variation of the bread and butter system.

Skilled metal workers may prefer to construct the hull from sheet metal rivetted or soldered to metal ribs, or to faithfully follow the details of full size practice and represent each plate and frame separately. Metal hulls are not recommended to the novice as they call for much greater skill and technique than a simple wooden hull.

Small hulls can be made very successfully with cardboard, and an example is illustrated in Chapter VI. Another effective method for small hulls is to model them in plaster, a method that is productive of good results, but the resulting hull is heavy and to some extent fragile, and there are difficulties with the fixing of small parts.

Concrete, ebonite, ivory, amber, tortoiseshell and numerous other materials have been used from time to time for the hulls of model boats, but the ship modeller is advised to leave them to those having the necessary skill and dexterity in their proper manipulation and application.

Taking everything into consideration the novice will be well advised to make the hull from wood, using good, dry, yellow pine for a solid block, sound pine or deal for a bread and butter hull, and mahogany or cedar for a planked hull, with oak, ash or elm for the ribs and keel.

Having decided upon the material and the method of construction, refer to the drawings and ascertain if any allowances will have to be made, for example:—

Suppose it is decided to make a hull from a solid block of wood, the best material would be dry yellow pine, ordinary deal if free from knots and blemishes could be employed, but to be suitable the block must be thoroughly dry, well seasoned, free from knots and cracks, reasonably straight and even in the grain. Commence operations by planing up the block on all four sides to the overall dimensions of the hull, then draw a line along the centre of its whole length, and draw other lines at right angles to it, spaced to correspond with the cross section lines on the design.

Continue these lines round the block on all four sides and number them in accordance with the design, as shown in fig. 51. Next mark on the upper surface the greatest breadth of the hull at each section line, noting that if there is any "tumble home" on the hull the greatest breadth may not be at the deck line or at the L.W.L. but at some other position, but in any case this will show on the body plan. On one of the sides of the block draw a line to represent the L.W.L. which will normally be horizontal, or parallel with the top surface. In cases where the bows are much higher than the stern or *vice versa* a saving of material can be effected by marking off the bow and stern heights and making the L.W.L. at an angle to the upper surface, but the section lines must always be at right angles to the L.W.L.

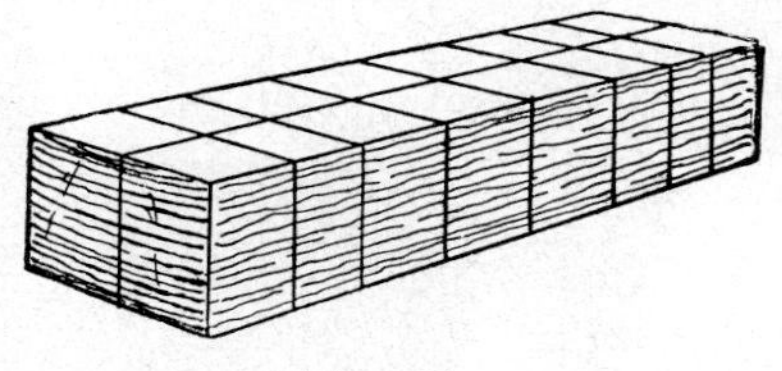

FIG. 51.
Section Lines drawn on the Wood Block.

Draw the outline of the profile or sheer plan on the sides of the block, and after making an allowance for cleaning up and finishing saw the block to shape, thus obtaining roughly the outline of the hull, as seen both in plan and in elevation. It will save trouble to have the block cut out at the local saw-mill, otherwise it must be done with a frame or bow saw. Plane up the block to the correct shape both in plan and elevation and then start shaping the outside. The best way of doing this is by screwing a block of wood to the top or deck side of the hull block and gripping it in a vice; an alternative is to bolt it to the bench by passing two coach screws through holes drilled through the bench and screwing them into the hull after packing blocks of wood have been placed under the hull to raise it above the bench. Be particular to keep the hull block level, or so placed that the L.W.L. is horizontal, and that the centre line of the hull is upright or square with the bench. Chisel off a portion of the block about midway of its length and test the shape by applying a mould or template to the hull as shown in fig. 82, Chapter VIII. Moulds are readily made from stout cardboard, and are prepared by drawing the centre line and the waterlines shown on the body plan. Then with dividers (or with proportional compasses as in fig. 52 if the drawing has to be enlarged or reduced) take off the various distances from the centre line along the horizontal lines to the curve of that section and mark them on their corresponding places on the mould.

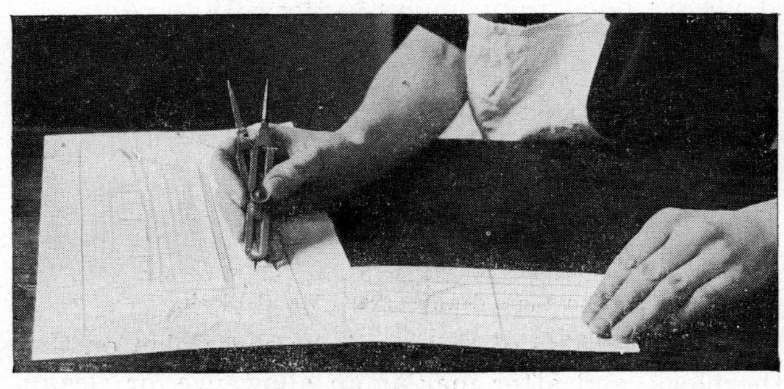

FIG. 52.
Using Proportional Compasses to Enlarge a Design.

Draw a fair curve through the spots thus determined and cut the card to the line, also cut the card exactly along the centre line and trim up the other edges making them square at all corners.

Make a mould for each important cross section on the body plan, number them clearly, and also ink in the L.W.L. so that it shows clearly. Make all these cardboard moulds the same external size and keep the L.W.L. on each at the same distance from the bottom edge of the card as this facilitates their use.

The mould must be applied to the hull in a vertical position, with the L.W.L. on the card, opposite to the L.W.L. on the hull, otherwise distortion may arise. When the hull is finally shaped, each mould should fit exactly to the surface of the hull at its proper station, and the central edge of the mould should then register with the centre line of the hull; and the L.W.L. on the mould and that on the hull should also be in register.

The moulds should be used from time to time as the hull is gradually shaped by cutting away the surplus timber. A good plan is to cut broad grooves around the hull and to roughly fit the midship section mould, and then to cut similar grooves for one or two sections near the bow and stern

FIG. 53.
Shaping the Bows with Spokeshave.

and to carefully chisel off the surplus wood between them. Work on both sides of the hull to about the same extent at each stage and continue carving the hull in this way, testing the shape at each section as the work progresses.

Diagonal cuts with the chisel, plane or spokeshave will help to prevent the formation of flats or ridges especially if the spokeshave is worked as in fig. 53, with broad easy strokes from amidships towards the bow or stern. The shaping can be further effected with coarse sandpaper applied with a brisk circular action and completed with long sweeping strokes using a pad of finest grade sandpaper, or preferably a piece of worn and old paper of a medium grade. While working on the hull it is necessary to keep the L.W.L. visible and if need be it should be re-drawn on the hull.

If the interior is to be hollowed, remove as much of the surplus wood as possible with the aid of a centre bit or auger, and carve out the remainder with broad gouges. During these operations it is advisable to support the hull in two blocks of wood shaped to fit the exterior at positions about one-fourth of the length of the hull from the bow and stern. Mount the supporting pieces securely on a base bar of stout timber and fix the hull to it with screws at any point where they will not be in the way, nor the screw holes show on the finished work. The bar can then be held in the vice or bolted to the bench and the hollowing out continued until the walls of the hull are about 1/8 in. to 3/16 inch thick, and somewhat thicker at the gunwale or upper edge, and at the bow and stern; the thickness of the hull can be measured with a large pair of calipers, those fitted with a graduated quadrant being the best.

Should the hull be accidentally damaged by driving a chisel through it, cut out the bad place and fit a new piece of wood securely into the hole and fasten it with strong shellac varnish or other adhesive, and when it has set hard shape the new piece to the contour of the hull.

After completing the hollowing process remove the hull from the support, when it may be found to have sprung and become narrower or wider (especially at the midship sections) than it should be. Find out if this is so or not, and at the same time test for "winding" by placing a straight-edge along the centre line from the bow to the stern, and measure the widths at each section when, if the hull is correct, the length of each half of any one section measured from the centre line to the hull side should be equal. If the walls of the hull have sprung inwards the trouble can be rectified when the deck beams are fitted, as they must be made to their correct dimensions and not merely to fit into the hull. To ascertain the length for any deck beam, measure the thickness of the hull at each side, deduct the thicknesses from the true width of the hull and make the beam that length. For example, if the deck width was 8 ins. and the hull $\frac{1}{4}$ in. thick on each side the deck beam would have to measure $7\frac{1}{2}$ in. long, consequently when a beam is fitted to the hull it will ensure the correct width at that section. Deck beams should be cambered, as shown on the designs, and preferably have knee pieces at the ends as indicated in fig. 54.

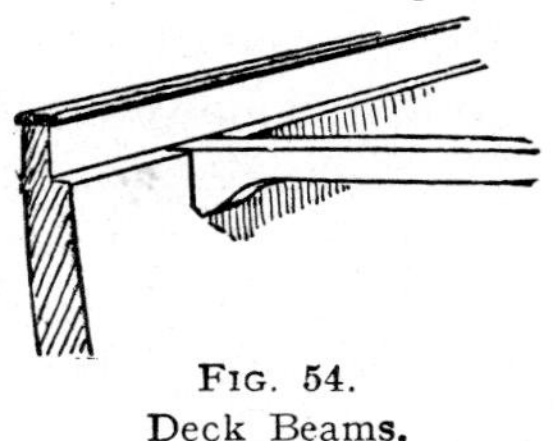

Fig. 54.
Deck Beams.

Deck beams finish flush with the upper edge of the hull if the deck is to be fitted on to the hull sides, but if the deck is recessed into the hull, to represent the bulwarks, then the beams must be lowered accordingly and an allowance made for the thickness of the deck to ensure the correct bulwark heights. Deck beams may be of mahogany or oak, and nominally about $\frac{1}{4}$ in. deep for the average hull, and can be secured with glue and a fine brass screw or pin driven from the outside of the hull.

The camber or transverse curvature of the deck is controlled by the deck beams, but it must also be a fair curve on the longitudinal centre line of the hull to ensure that the deck will fit nicely and present a neat appearance. Decks are preferably made from thin yellow pine, white sycamore, or maple with black pencil or ink lines to represent the planking. These lines should be ruled with a straight-edge, be parallel to the centre line and terminated at a line drawn a little way from the edge of the hull to represent the cover board. The hull should be given a good coating of shellac varnish on the inside if it has been hollowed, and the exterior painted with any suitable undercoating as described in Chapter XIV., Painting and Finishing.

So far no mention has been made of hulls for a model clipper that is intended to be sailed on a pond or on the sea, as in practice it is seldom that a boat of this kind is successful.

There are a few notable exceptions, but the models have had to be considerably modified and are necessarily simplified in the details of the sails and rigging. The underlying reason for the non-success of a practical sailing model of a clipper ship is that when a model is made to scale the hull is reduced in volume proportionally by the cube of the scale, whereas the sail area is reduced proportionally only by the square of the scale, hence the sail area is disproportionately large for the hull; moreover, the wind pressure remains the same at any given moment and place either for a model or for a real ship.

Readers who desire to make a working model will therefore have to be prepared to sacrifice appearance and proper scale proportions, consequently the result can at best be little more than a caricature although to the uninitiated it may appear a pleasing and accurate model.

If such a model must be made, then let it be as large as is practicable, say with a hull length of 5 to 6 feet, the beam and depth increased by about 10 per cent. over the correct scale proportions, the hull be made as light as possible and fitted with a deep metal fin keel and a lead bulb at the lowest part. The standing rigging must be securely fitted, and the running rigging and blocks well arranged and as simple in disposition as possible but will otherwise follow the lines described in this book. It would also be necessary to provide reefs or other means for quickly shortening sail when the wind increases in strength.

There is a fascination in this work for those who care to undertake a certain amount of experimentation, and anything in the nature of a race for working model clipper ships would be vastly entertaining and instructive.

CHAPTER VI.

PLANK BUILT HULLS.

Similar to the Foregoing but Dealing in Full Detail with Rib and Plank Built Hulls, and also with Partly Planked Hulls to Exhibit the Internal Construction of Actual Ships—Illustrated with Detailed Line Drawings and Photographs.

Built hulls comprise those which are made with a keel, or backbone, cross members or ribs, longitudinal curved members, known as strings, and wales, and clothed on the exterior with separate planks, completed and stiffened by beams, knees and so forth.

Actually in many models the construction is simplified as compared with full size practice, but when historical accuracy, or extreme attention to details are paramount considerations, it is practicable to exactly simulate full scale practice in a comparatively small model.

No hard and fast rules can be laid down as to the smallest practical size for a plank built hull, it depends so largely on the skill of the builder. Some excellent examples, only a few inches in length, are to be seen in exhibitions and private collections, but the amateur without previous experience will be well advised to consider a hull about 30 ins. long as the minimum for practical work.

Plank-building a small hull is unlike any other work, and calls for great patience and some amount of dexterity and technical skill, mostly it is a matter of patience and getting each part perfect at the start.

Before commencing actual work it will be well to visualise

the parts and become familiar with their nomenclature, and with this in view a study of fig. 55 showing the usual pieces in a model will be distinctly helpful. In this diagram, which is partly cut away to reveal otherwise hidden pieces, the keel is shown at *A*, knee at *B*, rib *C*, stem *D*, inwale *E*, breasthook *F*, gunwale *G*, fashion-piece *H*, beam *J*, toprail *K*, bulwarks *L*, and knight-head *M*.

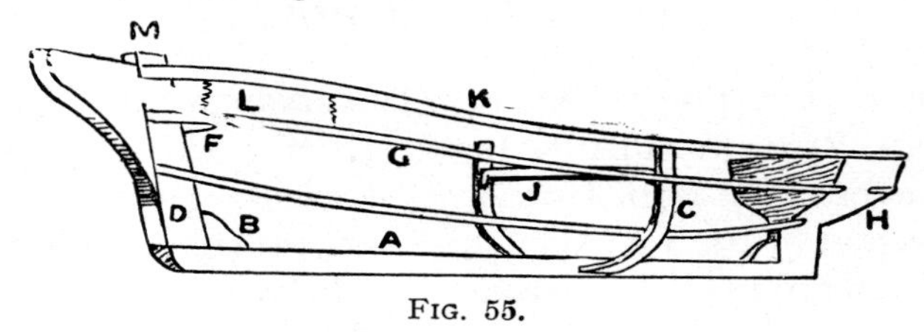

FIG. 55.
Names of Components of a Built Model Hull.

The only really practicable way to learn how to make a planked hull is to make one, and for a first essay in construction a little model in cardboard is economical, and while not exactly the same conditions are met as where working in wood, it will be found in practice that a few evenings spent on this work will teach more than anything else, and the practical experience is well worth having.

FIG. 56.
Clipper Hull Built up from Cardboard.

The underlying requirements of any form of built hull are a central frame or keel, disposed length-ways, a series of shaped members or ribs arranged at right angles to the central member, and a stiffener or two in the form of longitudinals.

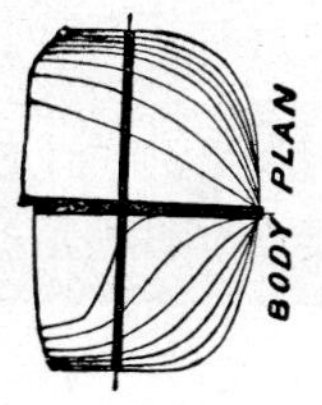

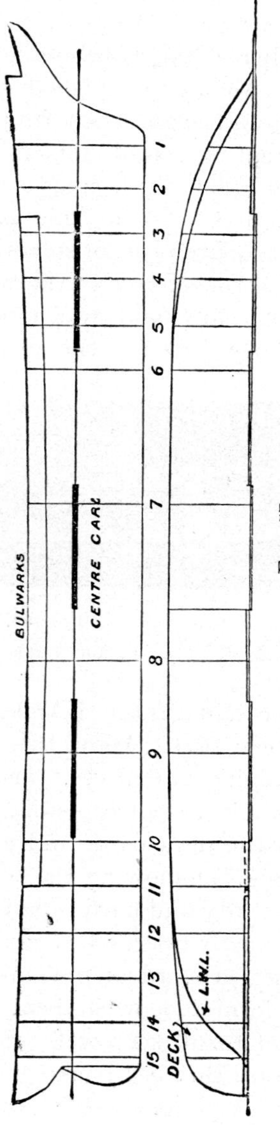

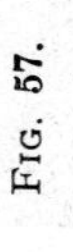

FIG. 57.
Lines of a Model Clipper Ship.

These in the cardboard model, seen in fig. 56, are represented by solid segments, or ribs, attached to a solid profile or keel, and strengthened by the deck members, and by a shaped member at the waterline level (L.W.L.)

The cards should be of good grade, and about No. 6 ply in thickness, and are set out from the designs, as shown in fig. 57 and cut to exact outside shape. The various slots as shown by solid black lines are then cut away and the pieces assembled. To do this pin the centre member to one edge of a square piece of smooth wood, and set the L.W.L. line flush with the surface of the wood. Then insert one half of the L.W.L. card, and add a few of the ribs. When the adhesive is dry, reverse the centre member and similarly

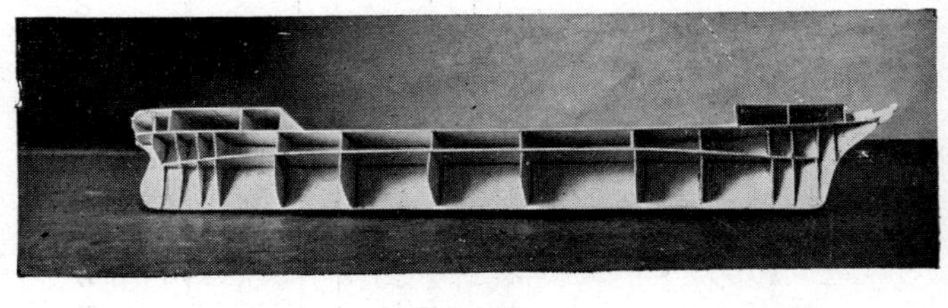

FIG. 58.
Hull with Rib and Deck Cards Assembled.

fix the other half of the L.W.L. card, and add the other portions of the ribs. Allow them to set hard and then fix all the remaining rib pieces, each of which will be in four parts and should be correspondingly numbered. When they are dry add the deck card, and also the poop and forecastle decks as in fig. 58 showing the work at this stage. As soon as the whole is dry and hard rub over the edges with sandpaper to ensure perfectly bevelled edges, and commence the planking by fixing the garboard or bulwark strake, which may appear of peculiar form but when bent into position as in fig. 59 will be found to fit very well. Some slight final truing will be needed, but this is covered by subsequent attention with sandpaper. A single piece arranged in this way is a convenient method of representing the bulwark and upper part of the hull sides.

FIG. 59.
Testing the Correctness of Bulwark Strake.

The next part to fit is the garboard strake, or that one which fits against the keel; this must be a curved piece, and to find its proper shape is to practically solve the problem of plank building.

For instance, if a straight plank be laid over the ribs as in fig. 60, the ends will be found to drop, when the hull is keel

FIG. 60.
A Single Straight Plank.

uppermost as shown, and obviously it would leave gaps at bow and stern. This is corrected by using a plank which curves upwards at the ends as shown in fig. 61. The actual shape of such plank is determined by that of the ribs, as the plank must lay flat and easily on each rib, and is in consequence twisted in its length, which twist has to be allowed for in the shape of the plank. It is only by trial and error that a perfect fit can be assured; there is no practical way of ascertaining exactly the shape of each, but some labour is saved by cutting a second plank to the pattern of the first, using it for the other half of the hull. Each half should be planked alternately, plank by plank to avoid straining the structure.

Fasten the plank temporarily with pins as in fig. 61 or

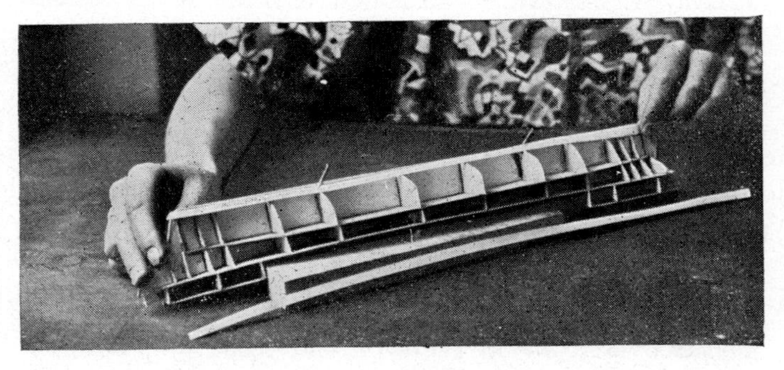

FIG. 61.
Fitting the Garboard Strake.

fine tacks, and prepare the next plank, which will be curved, but rather less than the first. Fit this as before, so that the edges of both planks make perfect contact, but on the cardboard model it will suffice if the edge of the second plank slightly overlaps the first. Continue in this way until the planks commence to run into the counter, when the shape of the plank will alter somewhat and have a somewhat hooked end as shown in fig. 62, which for purposes of the illustration is shown rather wider than usual and somewhat emphasized in shape. Similarly shaped planks are used to complete the planking, the last being tucked under the lower edge of the bulwark strake.

When dry, the exterior is smoothed with sandpaper, and the beads added to the bulwark strip as seen on the finished hull in fig. 56, which is a cardboard model 18 ins. long made in this way.

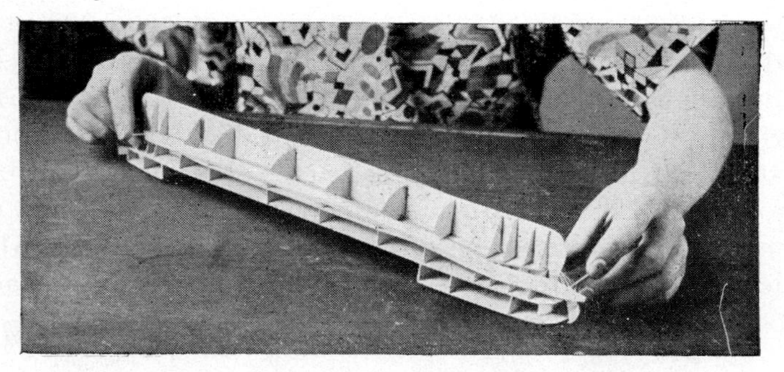

FIG. 62.
Form of a Plank for the Counter.

On this hull the figure-head is cut from thick card, modelled slightly with a sharp knife and then gummed and placed

FIG. 63.
Fixing the Figure-head.

in position as shown in fig. 63, and when this is dry the side pieces or stringers are gummed in place, fig. 64 showing this operation. This part is usually ornamented with carving or scroll work represented in a small model of this kind by paintwork, or with Gesso or similar modelling material.

This method makes a capital little hull, and has the merits of economy of material cost and only needs a sharp pair of scissors, knife and adhesive, and pins for its construction, and when painted is indistinguishable from a wooden hull and quite as durable for a show model. To make the surface perfectly smooth and to eliminate the ridges when so desired, paste small pieces of thin paper across the planks until the whole hull is covered, then sandpaper them smooth and add a second covering as before, fixed with shellac varnish, which when dry and sandpapered smooth yields a beautiful surface.

FIG. 64.
Fixing the Stringers.

When building in wood, exactly the same principles are followed but with a few modifications and additions, as may be judged from the following.

There are numerous differences of detail in the methods of the work, but the following gives satisfactory results. First make a set of shadows or moulds and mount them on a longitudinal bar spaced to correspond with each section shown on the lines. A shadow is made for each section on the body plan but less the thickness of both the rib and plank. The L.W.L. line must be marked on each shadow and be absolutely level one with the other. Fix the shadows to the bar by screws or in any secure manner, so that they can be readily removed later on, and if any sections have a "tumble home," that is, are wider anywhere than at the deck line, make the shadows in two pieces to facilitate removal, also cut the needful slots for the keel, inwales and the like.

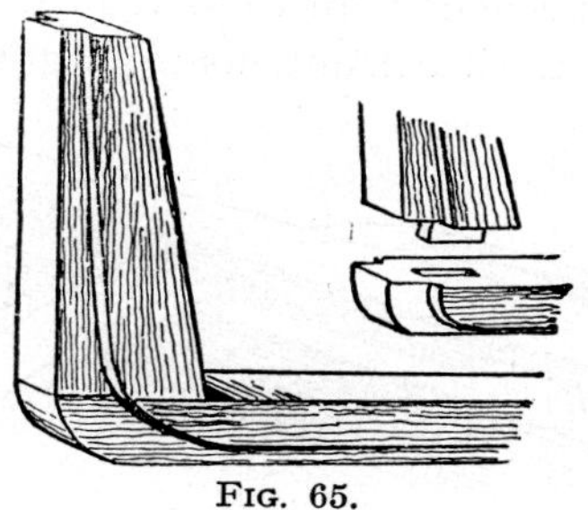

Fig. 65.
Stem-piece Mortised into Keel.

The next thing is to make a keel, with stem and sternpost, or counter or fashion-piece according to the needs of the design. This is best made of mahogany of suitable thickness and to mortise the stem-piece into the keel to give additional strength, fig. 65 shows a typical keel. Slots have next to be cut into the shadows at their centre to allow the keel-piece to drop into place, and can be cut before the shadows

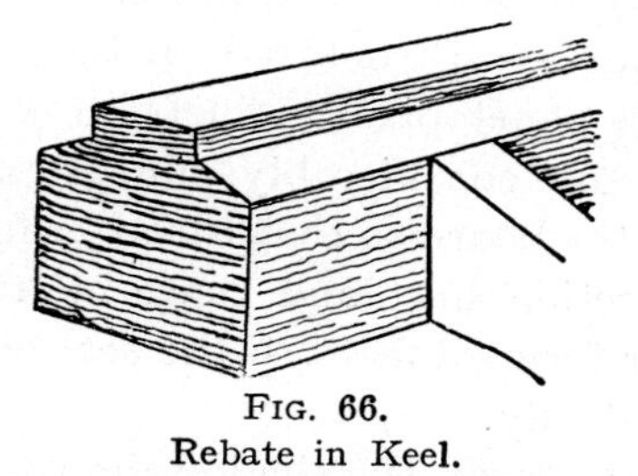

Fig. 66.
Rebate in Keel.

are finally fixed to the bar. The keel-piece should conform to the exact profile of the hull and must project above the shadows by at least the thickness of the ribs and planks. A rebate has to be cut into each side of the keel for the planks to fit into as indicated in cross section in fig. 66, and should be broad enough to support the plank. The curvature should allow the planks to lie flat and true and without unwanted twists.

The ribs may be made of oak or ash steamed and bent to fit tightly over the edge of the shadows, and, wherever the shape allows, it is an excellent plan to pierce the keel and pass the rib through and make it continuous from gunwale to gunwale.

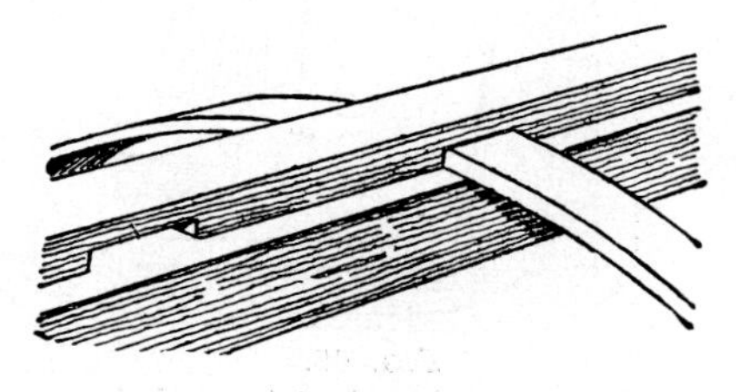

FIG. 67.
Joggle through the Keel.

The notch or joggle as it is called is shown in the keel in fig. 67, but where the shape is too acute to allow of the rib passing through the keel a somewhat similar notch or step is cut but is not pierced right through.

The ribs cut to suitable lengths are steamed in a fish kettle for a couple of hours, and will then be found to bend quite easily. They are then fitted on the shadows, temporarily secured with panel pins and left to dry. The sections forward and aft are considerably curved, and the shadows have to be set on the board so that the after face of the shadow is on the true section line, and those on the after sections are set with their forward faces to the section lines, and those amidships set centrally.

The square corners on the shadows must be shaped to the longitudinal curvature of the hull, which may easily be done with a rough file or fine cabinet rasp, and tested with a batten used in the same way as a plank.

Now prepare two inwales made of pine, mahogany or oak,

curved to suit the sheer line and fitted inside the ribs as fig. 68 at *A*, and checked into the stem and fashion-piece,

FIG. 68.
Inwales fitted to the Ribs.

as in fig. 69, which shows the inwales *A* checked into the rebate *B* cut in the fashion-piece *C* to receive the planks, and also shows the keel *D*, and knee *E*, attaching it to the solid wood of the fashion-piece. Note that the fashion-piece will be a solid block and shaped as if it were the stern part

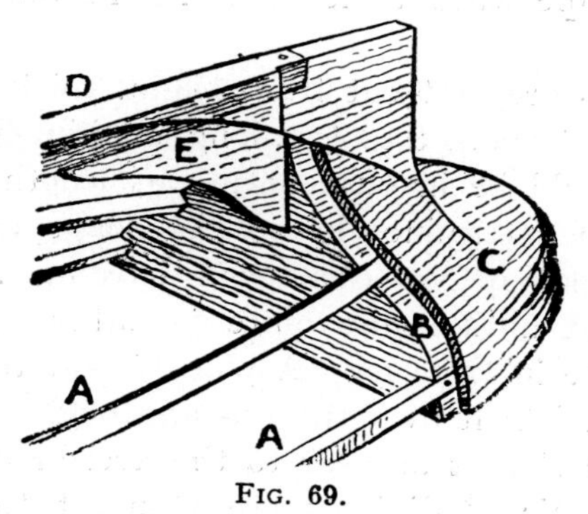

FIG. 69.
Inwales and Fashion-Piece.

of a solid block or carved hull. The inwale is best located on a level corresponding to the underside of the maindeck, and the ribs are consequently extended above it to provide support for the top rail bulwarks, poop or forecastle deck and so forth according to the details of the particular design.

The purpose of the inwale is to stiffen and support the ribs and provide something to support the deck beams.

After the ribs are dry and set, mark them for identification purposes and remove them from the shadows. Then permanently fasten the inwales by gluing and screwing them to the stem and fashion-piece, replace the ribs, glue and fasten them with fine brass screws to the keel and to the inwales, but be careful not to fasten them to the shadows, and sandpaper their faces to ensure a perfect bed for the planks.

There are differences of opinion as to the best way to plank a hull, but the important thing to remember is that the joints between each plank must fit, and must butt tightly against one another without forcing. If the planks are fitted properly most of the ribs will have the same number of planks, but of different widths except sometimes those at the bow and stern. An important matter is that the planks are not forced either up or down, as if they are the hull will change its shape when removed from the building bar and shadows.

The planks are best cut from 1/8-in. thick mahogany or cedar for a boat about 3 to 4 ft. long, or thinner for a smaller boat, and should be in one continuous length from bow to stern; and to determine the correct shape for each plank prepare a thick paper or cardboard pattern. A strip of the material is cut until it lies quite smoothly and fits snugly into the rebate in the keel. A plank is cut to the shape of the pattern and bent over the ribs and held in position with a few pins or clamps as near to the keel or other plank as possible. A pair of dividers are then set to the greatest distance from keel to plank and with them a line is scribed on the plank with one leg of the dividers while the other runs in the rebate. This line will indicate almost the exact shape for the edge of the plank, and if it is fashioned to this line and then offered up it will only need a very little work with a small plane or sandpaper to make a perfect fit.

To obtain the shape of the other edge of the plank draw a fair curve increasing or diminishing as needed at each end and cut the plank to this curve, when it will be ready for use. When one plank has been shaped, cut another one from it for use on the opposite side of the hull. Fix the first plank, securing it with shellac varnish and fine copper or brass pins, one through each rib, but use small brass screws into the stem and fashion-piece. Fit the corresponding plank on the opposite half and proceed to fit plank No. 2. A paper pattern can be made as before, or a strip of the planking can be bent to shape with one edge overlapping the first plank, as in fig. 70.

Fig. 70.
Preparing the Second Plank.

Hold it with cramps which may be strong paper clips or the like, and run a pencil along it from the inside of the hull, keeping the pencil close up to No. 1 plank. This gives the correct shape for that edge, and the other edge can be marked off as before.

The plank can then be cut to shape and tried in place, and adjusted until it fits perfectly, by planing off any inaccuracies. Prepare and fit all the other planks in the same way. Always endeavour to keep the planks in as fair and easy a curve as possible, and free from any suspicion of straining. Before the gunwale plank or top strake is finally fitted the spaces between the ribs must be filled in by gluing strips of pine to the faces of the inwales to fill the gaps, and to provide a fair face for the plank to fit against. It is preferable to fit these strips rather than use a thicker inwale with slots cut in for the ribs, as, if this done, the inwale will have a series of flats instead of being in one continuous curve. The top strake should be nailed right through the ribs and inwale, and also one nail at least driven between the ribs, through the packing strips and inwale.

Now go over the outside of the hull with glasspaper, remove any high places or edges on the planks, and give the whole a good coat of shellac varnish and allow it to set hard.

Afterwards turn the boat right side up and remove the building bar by unfastening the screws from the shadows. Fit a breast hook or > shaped knee to the hull at the stem as shown in fig. 71, which can be cut from oak or elm, and

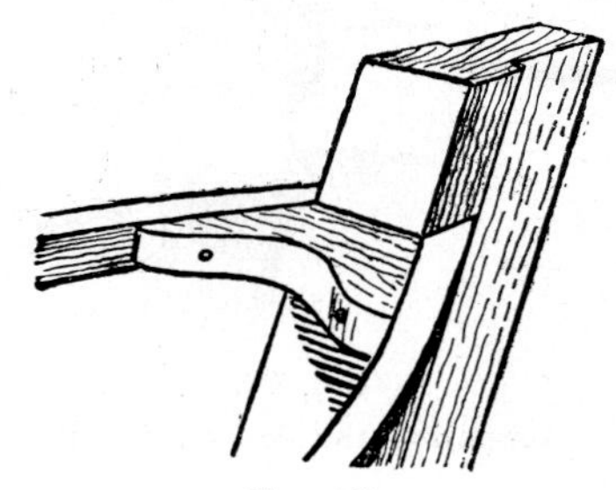

Fig. 71.
Breast-Hook fitted to the Stem.

should be glued and screwed in place; its purpose is to bind the top strake and inwales to the stem head and generally to strengthen the hull. Several deck beams are required to bind the hull together and prevent it changing shape while the shadows are removed.

These may either be permanent or temporary, the former, properly cambered to suit the deck, the latter can be simple pieces of lath temporarily tacked in position and removed after the proper deck beams are fitted. Their construction is dealt with in Chapter V., page 57.

Remove the shadows by gentle coaxing, or if necessary

by cutting a piece out of them with a keyhole saw and after removal clench over any protruding nails and give the interior of the hull two coats of shellac varnish. The deck beams can then be fitted as well as the other items, such as cabins and bulkheads according to the requirements of the design and further dealt with in Chapter X. dealing with deck erections.

The same methods are followed in greater detail when it is desired to reproduce every detail of a regular ship construction, but in that case the ribs are sawn to shape from flat board of appropriate thickness and gradually built up in several pieces, exactly as in a real hull, and a far larger number of ribs, floors and other timbers are required. In all practical model work they can however be omitted.

Another item that can be dealt with in greater detail is the counter, which can be entirely built up in ribs and planked, as in a real ship.

A composite hull can be modelled with metal frames and timber planking by cutting the frames to shape and generally building them up with tinplate soldered together. Similarly a metal hull can be made with metal ribs, keel, etc., and plated with separate sheets of tinplate, copper or brass, but it is doubtful if it is either desirable or practical for the novice.

CHAPTER VII.

MODELLING THE "LOCH TORRENS."

COMMENCING THE WORK ON A FOUR-MASTED BARQUE RIGGED CLIPPER CHARACTERISTIC OF THE PRACTICE DURING THE PERIOD 1881 TO 1885—TOOLS NEEDED AND HOW TO USE THEM—LISTS OF MATERIALS AND SOURCES OF SUPPLY—ILLUSTRATED WITH LINE DRAWINGS, PHOTOGRAPHS AND FOLDING PLATES.

THE model bearing this title forms the chief subject matter of the next few chapters, and in many respects can be taken as a typical example of the splendid results that are possible by amateur craftsmen. Every part of this model illustrated in fig. 72 and plates Nos. 1 to 5 has been made by amateurs to ship modelling, with very simple implements, using everyday materials readily procurable in all localities. It would of course be ridiculous to suppose that novices could make a ship model which could equal the magnificent pieces of craftsmanship turned out by the big commercial firms specialising in this work employing specially trained and well skilled mechanics, and with all the resources of a fully equipped workshop.

The *Loch Torrens* is, however, a well made model and would hold its own in any competition for amateur ship modelling, and no excuses are made for it or its builders.

A large number of specially prepared photographs have been secured showing the progress of the work in detail to stimulate and guide other novices desirous of turning out a worth while model—something that is to scale, that reproduces most of the rigging details and is fairly complete in

PLATE 1.—ABOVE WATER PROFILE OF *LOCH TORRENS.*

Inserted in "How to Make Clipper Ship Models," Brown, Son & Ferguson, Ltd.

[To Face Page 74

FIG. 72.—Starboard Quarter View of *Loch Torrens.*

equipment. Readers who have successfully made either of the models described in the previous chapters can undertake the work on the *Loch Torrens* in the full assurance that the methods described will enable them to turn out a duplicate, at least as good, and possibly better. The fullest information is given in the form of working drawings, photographic illustrations, and pen sketches of the original, and by carefully following them a splendid result should be attained.

There are no hard and fast rules for success in modelling the *Loch Torrens* or any other ship model, neither is there one and one way only in which the work can be done, but the methods described are known to be successful, and moreover, are applicable by any ordinary person with a rudimentary knowledge of constructional work.

First of all it must be realised that it takes a long time to complete a model of this kind, probably of the order of six months when working a few hours of an evening, on Saturdays, and generally under the usual conditions of amateur work. There is very little in the way of "mess" occasioned by the work and it can therefore be carried on in any ordinary living room, especially if a few boxes of convenient size be allocated as storage places for the parts and tools as most of the pieces are quite small and therefore easily lost.

Roughly speaking, the order in which the work is done is, first make the hull, then the masts and spars, next prepare the more important deck fittings. After this the masts are assembled and partly rigged, the yard ironwork made and fitted, the masts stepped and the standing rigging set up. This stage is followed by the fitting out, fixing the remaining rigging, and the bending of the sails; lastly, the remaining details are added and the case and stand constructed as an appropriate protection for the finished work.

For the convenience of those who may desire to model some other type of clipper, the subject matter of the chapter covering the *Loch Torrens* has been grouped into sections and additional information given to enable any desired amount of detail to be incorporated, or any other boat to be constructed.

It should be realised that a three-masted ship can be modelled on exactly similar lines to *Loch Torrens*, and many variations in rig can also be effected by adding or omitting the parts concerned. One point that must be studied carefully is the contemporary practice on shipboard. It is impossible to successfully apply all the details found in a ship of the period 1881 to a model representing a ship built, say, in 1860. For instance, it is incongruous to see the masts rigged in the fashion of, say, 1870 in a hull typical of the practice 15 years later. These points are, however, more likely to become apparent to the student and historian than to occasion great inconvenience to the ship modeller as the constructional methods in model work are very similar; it is more a matter of the arrangement of the rigging, proportions of sails, and the form of the hull, than differences in methods of making similar parts.

Another factor to bear in mind when modelling a particular ship is that during her useful and active life she may have been considerably modified in rigging details. First mates especially were prone to amend details in this way, quite as effectively as the master. An instance of this kind is that celebrated and famous clipper *Cutty Sark*—known the world over as a full rigged clipper ship—yet at one period of her career she was rigged as a barquentine; but any model maker who showed her in that guise would be likely to court unkind remarks from many who knew her only as a fully rigged ship.

Those who decide to make a model of any particular ship should therefore consider these matters carefully, and having ascertained the requisite details can with confidence adopt or adapt the constructional methods used in the building of *Loch Torrens*.

There is no prototype of *Loch Torrens*. She is a type, rather than an exact replica of a specific ship, but she represents with remarkable fidelity a class of clipper ship built in

Glasgow by Barclay, Curle & Co. about 1881, fine, fast sailing and graceful four masters, comfortable, well-found and good sea boats of the order of 280 feet in length with masts reaching to heights of over 180 feet, the sail plan and rigging designed for expeditious handling by a minimum crew. The hull, graceful and clean in design with a whale back forecastle and poop, was in the actual ships built of iron or steel, a material frequently adopted for the lower and topmasts.

Before starting work on *Loch Torrens* the constructor may wish to know the cost of materials and have some idea

FIG. 73.

Group of Tools and Materials used in making *Loch Torrens.*

of what tools are needed to carry out the work. The first item is practically negligible, the entire cost of all the materials including timber for the stand and glass for the showcase did not exceed twenty-five shillings; actually the outlay was less than this as much of the material was already available.

As regards the tools that are necessary—the following is a complete list of everything actually used in the construction of the model and most of them are shown in fig. 73.

Bow saw, used for cutting the hull timber, a keyhole saw could have been used, or it would have been quite practical to employ any ordinary hand saw, to cut the wood as nearly as possible to the shape and finish it with a chisel and spokeshave.

Small iron plane, costing only a few shillings, used for smoothing the timber and bringing it to correct thickness, for shaping spars and suchlike work. A chisel, $\frac{1}{2}$ in. wide, employed for shaping the hull, a wider one would be useful in addition, and a small flat gouge, but neither of the latter was actually used on the work.

Small spokeshave, measuring about 6 inches in total length, very handy when working on the exterior of the hull,

FIG. 74.
Using the Spokeshave.

especially at the bow and stern. This tool comprises a central cutter or blade adjustably mounted on a hardwood body with hand grips at each end, and used by grasping it with both hands, with the cutting edge of the blade away from the body, and pushing it over the work with a light sweeping motion. By suitable movements of the two wrists and arms the implement can be made to travel in a curved path and thus greatly assist in the production of a gracefully curved hull. This action and the proper way of manipulating the spokeshave is illustrated in fig. 74, and the novice is advised to acquire a similar specimen and practise with it on a spare piece of wood to attain some dexterity before using it on the actual model.

The spokeshave, like the chisel and gouge, must be kept exceedingly sharp, with a keen cutting edge, accomplished by rubbing on an oil-stone slip. To do this the blade of the spokeshave is loosened by light blows with a hammer on the spurs or peg-like ends of the blade which fit tightly into holes in the body and then to press it out as shown in fig. 75 with

FIG. 75.
Removing Blade of Spokeshave.

the thumbs. Chisels, plane irons and similar cutting tools are sharpened in a somewhat similar manner pictured in fig. 76, by pushing the blade backward and forwards along the stone, keeping the blade always at the same inclination. The bevelled or sloping side is applied to the stone during the major portion of the time, but the last few strokes are made by laying it flat on the stone, with the bevel side upwards, to remove a slight raggedness which usually forms on that edge. Keep the oil-stone at hand and whenever any cutting tool gets dull and will not cut freely enliven it by a few strokes on the stone. Keen edged cutting tools are the greatest possible aid, but remember to place them carefully on the bench, do not let their cutting edges overhang the edge or an accident may follow. Always work with the cutting edge away from the body and never press a cutting tool towards the hands, otherwise it will only be a question of time before a nasty accident happens. A very small

Fig. 76.
Sharpening the Chisel.

hammer, weighing only an ounce or so, is essential, as are cutting nippers for clipping off wire and very thin metal strips; a long-nosed pair of pliers, also small, are invaluable.

Fig. 77.
Punching a Hole with Square Bradawl.

Other tools employed include a small, cheap hand drill, and a few drill bits, small crotchet hook used on the rigging and several needles of various sizes. A square bradawl, shown in use in fig. 77, is most handy; it has a very sharp point and is employed for making holes in wood, metal or cardboard or for enlarging holes. To pierce metal, proceed as in the illustration by placing the metal on a knot in a piece of odd wood, hold the bradawl erect and strike the top of the handle a light blow with the hammer to drive the point through the metal. Then revolve the bradawl by hand until the hole is sufficiently enlarged. A hole about the diameter of an ordinary pin is easily made in this way and is often preferable to drilling as the very small drills are fragile and easily broken. Soldering iron, flux, and solder are employed extensively in making up the various metal fittings, and it is well for the novice to acquire familiarity with the process of soldering. Really

FIG. 78.
Tinning the Soldering Iron.

it is very simple and easy but requiries a certain knack. The essentials are perfectly clean metal parts to be united, a properly heated iron—by "iron" is meant the copper bolt or bit at the end of the metal rod—and the use of suitable flux. The preparation known as "Fluxite" is most effective and convenient. It is a brown paste and a very little must be smeared on the parts to be soldered which can conveniently be applied with a pointed match stick. The first operation in soldering is to "tin the bit," which is done by heating the iron in a clear fire until it is nearly red hot, but never quite red hot.

Next rub the hot iron on a piece of rag or emery paper to clean the point, and then immediately press and slowly rotate it on a piece of clean tin smeared with Fluxite, and hold the stick of solder against it, as in fig. 78, which will cause the solder to melt and adhere to the end of the iron, which should then appear bright as if silver-plated. Only when the iron is in this condition is it possible to solder properly. To unite two pieces of metal first apply the flux, bring the parts into firm contact, then hold the hot iron on the parts to be jointed, apply the stick of solder to the iron, and as it melts draw the molten metal along by gradually moving the iron over the work. The molten solder always tries to run after the hot iron and consequently it can be made to flow in any direction by suitable manipulation of the iron. Do not use more flux or solder than is absolutely necessary; indeed on many little pieces the solder adhering to the point of the bit is generally sufficient.

The only other tools used in making *Loch Torrens* are a ruling pen for drawing ink lines on the deck and elsewhere, a large and small penknife, perhaps the most useful of all the tools, and a small round file, a 6-in. square file, 6-in. narrow flat file called a pillar file. A cabinet rasp and a riffler file were used as they were available, but are not essential; dividers, and proportional compasses for taking off the sizes of parts on the drawings, and the domestic wood saw for cutting the timber to length; Gillette razor blade for cutting the sails; screwdriver, scissors, square, snout-nosed pliers, rule.

Proportional compasses are very useful when making a model to a different scale or size than the available drawings, but they are expensive to buy, and to avoid this a special card-board scale can be made and used as described in Chapter XVI.

Paints and brushes, sandpaper and pieces of rag, while not properly classified as tools are of course necessary, as is a small bench vice of some kind for the purpose of holding various small parts. There is no objection to using a greater selection of tools, in fact a small turning lathe and equipment and a small high speed bench drill are most useful, and a number of other tools are likewise very handy. The point that the author wishes to emphasize is that only a few inexpensive and simple tools are absolutely necessary, and that with them a really good model can be made by any normal man or woman—for ship modelling is attractive to the fair sex, their natural neatness and familiarity with needlework is a definite asset in the pursuit of an interesting pastime.

The materials employed in the construction of *Loch Torrens* embrace the following, but others might be substituted.

Hull.—4 pieces of white deal 3⅝ ins. wide, 9/16 in. thick, 24 ins. long, 1 piece white deal 3⅝ ins. wide, 1⅛ ins. thick, 26 ins. long. These allow for subsequent planing to exact thicknesses.

Stand.—1 piece white deal 5½ ins. wide, ½ in. thick, 24 ins. long; 2 pieces for uprights 3¾ ins. wide, ⅜ in. thick, 3½ ins. long. Small piece of velvet for lining.

Masts and Spars.—Yellow pine—planed from square strips to requisite lengths and diameter.

Decks.—2-ply Bristol board.

Deck Erections.—3-ply Bristol board.

Ships' Boats.—Yellow pine ½ in. thick, carved as requisite.

Hand Rails.—1/16 sq. tinned copper wire and pins.

Metal Work generally.—20 gauge sheet zinc, a piece about 6 ins. square is ample, brass wire No. 22 gauge.

Blocks.—Boxwood, carved and drilled. Small beads.

Sails.—Fine crepe paper.

Anchors.—Ebonite sheet 1/8 in. thick, a piece about 3 ins. square.

Rigging.—Black cotton thread, bouquet or floral wire, No. 28 gauge D.C.C. wire as used in wireless work.

Show Case.—Frame made from "stripwood." Stand yellow deal.

Paints.—Metal work, eggshell black; hull, black, white, light gray, dark gray. Best coach colours ground in oil.

Varnish.—Best copal.

In addition, a large box of assorted pins, a few odds and ends of wood and card, a tube of seccotine, a very fine chain. from a toy watch or cheap jewellery, some tiny beads, panel pins 1 in. long and a few small screws and nails.

Last to be mentioned but first in importance are the working drawings, which will be found inserted in the pages of this book, in the form of folding plates.

Each plate has been prepared to show a particular section of the work, and collectively they give all necessary information when supplemented by the diagrams in the text.

A few words in conclusion concerning sources of supply may be helpful.

Timber.—Is best obtained from the timber yard, and a courteous enquiry coupled with a gratuity to the yardman will almost always ensure getting well chosen and dry material free from knots and splits.

Bristol Boards.—Are obtainable from stationers and dealers in artists' materials.

Metal.—Usually the ironmonger or wireless dealer can supply, otherwise send to any reputable dealer in model makers' supplies, mentioning this book and the purpose of the material.

Paints.—From any good oil and colour merchants or dealers in artists' materials.

Cotton, Silk and Thread.—From any drapery establishment.

CHAPTER VIII.

THE HULL AND STAND.

How to Make the Hull with Particular Attention to the Fitting up of the Decks and Other Details not Dealt with in the Chapters on Hull Construction—Making the Stand—Illustrated with Photographs and a Folding Plate.

The hull is rightly and naturally the first part of a ship to be made, and this procedure is equally appropriate with model work. In a previous chapter several methods of hull construction were reviewed, but in this particular attention is devoted to the bread and butter or laminated system, especially as applied to the hull for the *Loch Torrens*.

The scale selected for this model is one-twelfth of an inch to 1 foot which produces the following overall dimensions: —Length overall 30 ins., breadth overall $8\frac{1}{2}$ ins., height from stand to truck $16\frac{1}{2}$ ins. The hull dimensions are 26 ins. long overall, $3\frac{1}{2}$ ins. greatest beam, $3\frac{1}{8}$ ins. depth, and plate No. 2 gives the complete lines or working drawings.

All dimensions and particulars of the hull should be taken from this drawing because on the others the hull has only been approximately indicated.

All the drawings (plates Nos. 2 to 5) are reproduced exactly one half full size, which greatly simplifies the trouble of enlarging them, assuming that a model will be made to the above dimensions, but if built to a larger or smaller scale the drawings must be enlarged or reduced accordingly.

The "bread and butter system" is the most practical method of construction for the amateur to adopt if unable to undertake the very intricate and accurate work involved in building a hull with ribs and planks. A bread and butter or laminated hull consists of a number of planks or flat boards of convenient thickness each fashioned to the shape of a waterline and then fastened together one on top of the other, and fig. 79 gives an idea of the appearance of the hull of the *Loch Torrens* made on this system, and nearly completed

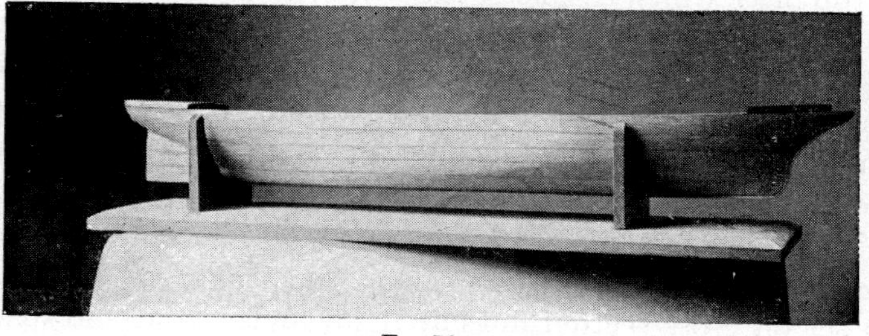

Fig. 79.
Hull and Stand

The best wood to employ is really sound, dry, yellow pine, failing which American bass wood or white wood will answer very nicely. Should it be desired to emphasise the lines of the hull, it is permissible to employ alternate layers of differently coloured woods, as for example, pine and mahogany or cedar, finished bright, that is clear varnished or polished.

Good grade bass wood is generally obtainable without difficulty but good yellow pine is much scarcer, but whatever material be selected the primary requisite is that the wood be thoroughly well seasoned and bone dry, or it will warp and shrink after the hull has been shaped.

On the score of economy it may be necessary to utilise ordinary commercial deal sold by builders' merchants, and in that event as dry and aged a piece as possible should be selected. Always use wood that is quite free from knots, as these being very hard have a tendency to project above the surface and cause the joints to open, but an otherwise good board with a knot in it can be used if the knot is well away from the edge, because it can then be cut out and the gap left in the wood.

Having obtained the timber, plane it to the exact thicknesses shown on the drawings between adjacent waterlines, the top plank is $1\frac{1}{16}$, the others are $\frac{1}{2}$ in. thick; take pains to get the surfaces truly level and make sure they are parallel. The wood has now to be marked out and a start is made on the top piece which is thicker than the others and reaches from the upper part of the hull to the first waterline, W^1 on plate No. 2. The shape to be drawn on this plank is nominally the deck plan, but actually it has to be as large as the greatest dimension at any point on any portion of the hull on or above the waterline W^1.

The upper face of the top plank should be marked out as follows. Draw a centre line along the length of the plank and set off cross section lines at right angles to it, and spaced to correspond with the cross section lines on the half breadth plan, plate No. 2. Along these lines, working outwards from the centre line, proceed to set off, on each side of the centre line, the greatest width at each section shown on the half breadth plan, and draw a fair curve through these spots.

Now proceed in a similar manner with the next piece of timber, which will reach from the waterline W^1 to the L.W.L., but in this case the widths to be set off at each cross section line are those shown on the half breadth plan plate No. 2, measured from the centre line to the curve of the waterline W^1. The remaining three pieces are then dealt with in a similar manner; the shape to be drawn on the upper surface of the third plank is derived from the curved line L.W.L. on the half breadth plan; the shape of the fourth plank from line W^2, and that of the bottom plank from line W^3. The lengths are to be marked off in a similar way, recording on the plank the greatest length found anywhere on or between the waterline under consideration, and the one above it.

The next operation is to saw the planks to shape with a bow saw as shown in fig. 80 or with a keyhole saw. Do not saw exactly on the line but a little to the waste side to allow for the subsequent shaping.

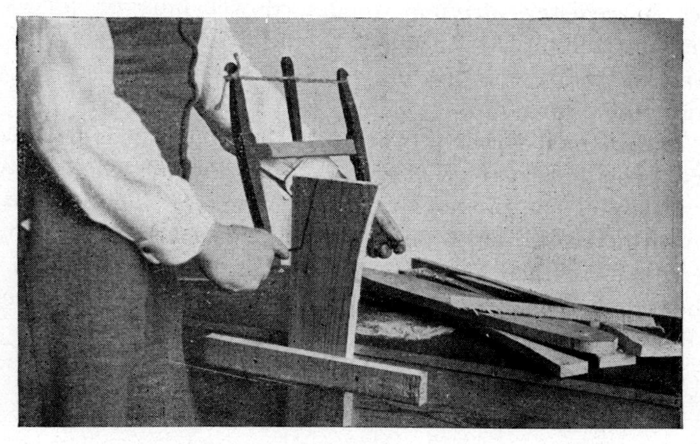

FIG. 80.

Sawing Planks to Shape.

An interesting and effective substitute for a carpenter's vice shown in fig. 80 consists of a stout batten of wood which clamps the work vertically to the side of the bench or table,

FIG. 81.

Planks Sawn to Shape.

a couple of stout screws being driven through the batten for this purpose. The edges of the sawn planks are next fashioned with a plane, chisel or spokeshave until they are square with the upper surface, and exactly shaped to the curved lines, and should then present somewhat of the appearance of fig. 81. Fasten all the planks together with all their centre lines in register, driving wooden dowel pins or pieces of round match sticks through them, after well glueing the surfaces, and then allowing the block thus formed to dry thoroughly hard.

The planks can be screwed together, but this is not necessary if the dowels are well driven home, and the whole allowed to set under the pressure of heavy weights. The advantage of well fitted dowels is that, should one of them accidentally pierce the surface, it will automatically be shaped with the other parts of the hull, whereas an accident with a metal screw is more difficult to deal with.

FIG. 82.
Testing the Shape with a Mould.

The outside has to be shaped in the same way as a solid hull by carving away the exterior as described in Chapter V. and as shown in fig. 82, and repeatedly testing the form with a mould. There is this important difference, however, between the bread and butter or laminated hull and the solid block hull: the edges of the laminations are known to be correctly shaped from the stern to the bow and it is only necessary to carve away the steps or corners, which is a much easier job than fashioning the shape from a solid block. Moreover, as the joint lines are true, there is no risk of the hull getting out of line or in "winding" as it is called.

The angular edges of the planks are most readily cut away by using the chisel in a diagonal manner as indicated in fig. 83, working always from the midship part towards the bow and stern, that is, cutting always in the direction of, or partially across, the grain of the wood.

FIG. 83.
Chiselling Diagonally across the Corners.

For most clipper models the hull block will be left solid, but if desirous of lightening it the surplus wood can be cut away with a keyhole or bow saw, prior to fastening the planks together. The permissible amount to be cut out is determined by assembling the planks in their proper positions and marking on the underside of each the shape of the outside of the plank beneath, and then cutting out the interior to within ½ in. or thereabouts of this line.

The planks are assembled, glued together and dowelled in the same way as before, and after the exterior has been shaped the inside is smoothened as far as possible by cutting away the angular edges with a broad and fairly flat gouge.

The fitting of decks, beams, and so forth follows similar procedure to that mentioned in Chapter VI. for other forms of hull construction. The hull of *Loch Torrens* has to be finished by recessing or carving out the wood on the top plank to a depth of about $\frac{1}{4}$ in. from the poop bulkhead to the forecastle, thus forming the bulwarks as shown in fig. 84. Two small pieces of timber each about $\frac{1}{4}$ in. thick are then

FIG. 84.
Hull showing Recessed Deck.

cut to shape and glued and pinned to the top plank to complete the poop and forecastle respectively and their edges are then rounded off to represent the whaleback, as is shown, on plates Nos. 1 and 5.

The keel is represented by a very small square sectioned strip of wood, 1/16 in. square, glued and pinned to the hull,

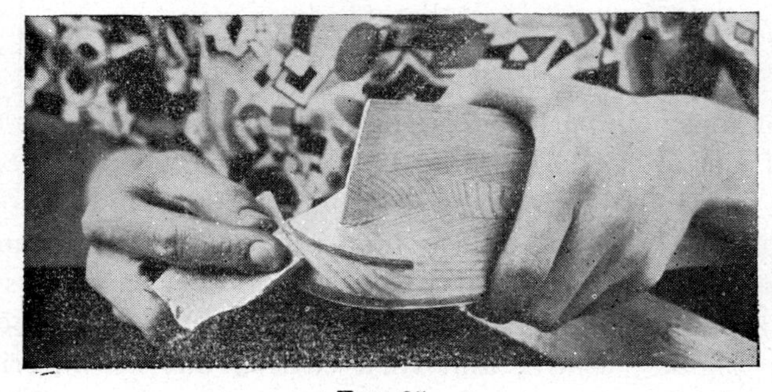

FIG. 85.
The Stern and Knuckle.

and extending from the stern to a little above the L.W.L. where it tapers into the turn of the stem head. Particular attention must be paid to the shaping of the bow and stern; the former should be a hollow curve, while at the stern the shape of the counter is important.

It is difficult to describe a shape in words but there should be a definite change of line in the counter, and this line of demarkation should be parallel with the upper edge of the hull. This line is called the knuckle and is emphasised in fig. 85 by the dark line on the hull, and should appear when finished as a little ridge or projection. It can be formed by carefully chiselling the wood in the vicinity and completing it by lightly sandpapering as shown in the illustration.

The whole of the hull should now be given a good rub down with fine sandpaper, and then be followed with an undercoating of suitable paint as described in Chapter XIV. on Painting and Finishing.

FIG. 86.
Fixing the Deck Card.

The next operations are to cut three pieces of 2-ply Bristol board to cover respectively the forecastle, poop and maindecks, the latter fitting neatly into the recessed portion. Those for the forecastle and poop have to be shaped to a curve to correspond with the outline of the hull, but finish at the upper turn of the whaleback, as is clearly visible in several illustrations (notably fig. 133 in Chapter X.). The poop and forecastle deck cards should have a line drawn on them with Indian ink, parallel with the outer edge and 1/8 in. from it, and the spaces so defined have lines about 1/16 in.

apart ruled on them parallel to the centre line to represent the planking. Paint the outer margin a warm brown to represent the teak cover boards, but leave the other parts white. These cards can then be gummed to the hull at any later and convenient time.

The maindeck card is similarly prepared but the brown edges or covering boards are omitted. This card can, however, be gummed to the surface of the hull and is temporarily secured by driving pins into the bulwarks as shown in fig. 86 to force the card into close contact with the wood of the hull.

Fig. 87.
Detail of the Rudder.

The rudder, although not an integral part of the hull, is referred to here for convenience, but it can actually be fixed with fine pins and seccotine at any later time as is most convenient.

The rudder is cut to shape from a piece of stout Bristol board, and narrow strips of thin card gummed to it to represent the metal straps for the hinges or pintles and eyes. Similar narrow strips of card have to be gummed to the hull to represent the straps, and should be located immediately beneath those on the rudder; these parts are clearly shown in fig. 87 where the rudder is being placed in position.

A simple stand should now be prepared on the lines shown in fig. 79, and may consist of a board 24 ins. long, 5½ ins. wide and ½ in. thick, to the upper surface of which are screwed two hardwood supports shaped at the top in conformity with the hull and their inner edges faced with strips of black velvet to avoid damage to the hull surface. This stand will be found very useful during the further work on the hull and rigging, but a more ornamental pattern can be prepared later on, in conjunction with the glass case as dealt with in Chapter XV.

CHAPTER IX.

MASTS AND SPARS.

EACH PIECE SEPARATELY ILLUSTRATED AND DESCRIBED, TOGETHER WITH THE NEEDFUL IRONWORK AND OTHER DETAILS, INCLUDING THE NECESSARY BLOCKS AND TACKLES—ILLUSTRATED WITH PHOTOGRAPHS AND LINE DRAWINGS OF DETAILS.

THE expression masts and spars is applied to all those metal or wooden parts which support the sails, and includes the masts, yards, booms, bowsprit and so forth. The appearance of the model is greatly influenced by the correctness or otherwise with which these parts are proportioned, consequently the masts and spars are a very important part of ship modelling.

Novices who inspect a well made commercial example of ship modelling may be excused for feeling disturbed by the lightness of the spars, and the apparent complexity of the various metal and other fittings associated with them. If, however, a reasonable amount of painstaking care be put into the work the amateur can rest assured that excellent results will follow the adoption of the hints in this chapter.

Evidence of what can be done by an amateur is given in fig. 88, an excellent example of a clipper ship model built by Mr. H. H. Marsden from designs by the author. This model has been further embellished by Mr. Marsden since the photograph was taken—by the addition of sails—but the picture shows clearly the importance of the sparring of a clipper ship model.

The materials usable for masts and spars are wood and brass, the former for preference, the latter for particularly fragile yards. A splendid example of metal masts and spars made by Messrs. Bassett-Lowke for *Cutty Sark* is shown in fig. 89 and the bowsprit and jibboom in fig. 90. The

FIG. 88.

Rigged Clipper Model Built by H. H. Marsden, Esq.

wood for masts and spars should be very evenly grained and nothing is better than good yellow pine, but any tough grained wood is permissible. Customarily on ship models the masts and spars are circular in cross section, particularly on models built to a smaller scale than $\frac{1}{4}$ in. to 1 foot, as although on a real ship the masts and spars have sundry battens—rubbing paunches and so forth—these when reduced to scale would be very small, and their omission is not a serious matter. As the *Loch Torrens* is quite small all the masts and spars are circular in cross section, but as closely to scale diameter, length, and taper as is feasible. The

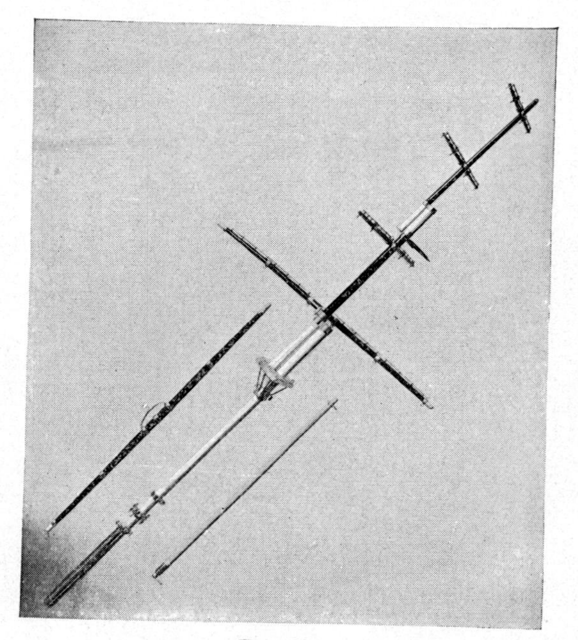

FIG. 89.
Metal Masts and Spars for *Cutty Sark.*

dimensions can be ascertained from the information given on plate No. 3 and this drawing should be adhered to in this respect, as where corresponding spars are shown in the other drawings they have only been approximately indicated for reference purposes.

Work should be commenced on the three lower masts,

and the first operation is to cut a piece of timber to length and plane it on all four sides to the correct taper, and to make

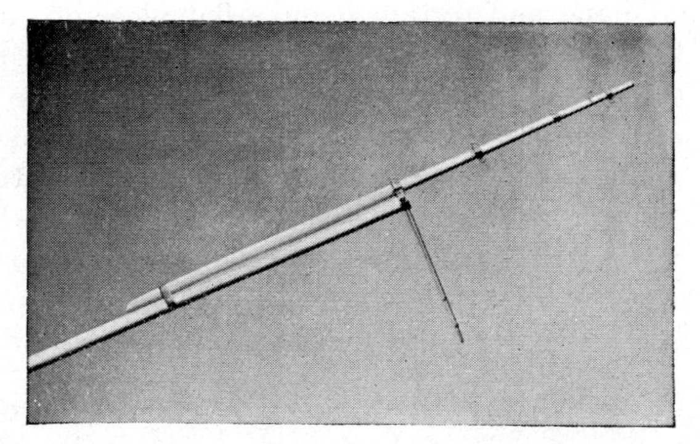

FIG. 90.
Bowsprit and Jibboom for *Cutty Sark.*

the widths across the flats correspond with the diameters given on plate No. 3.

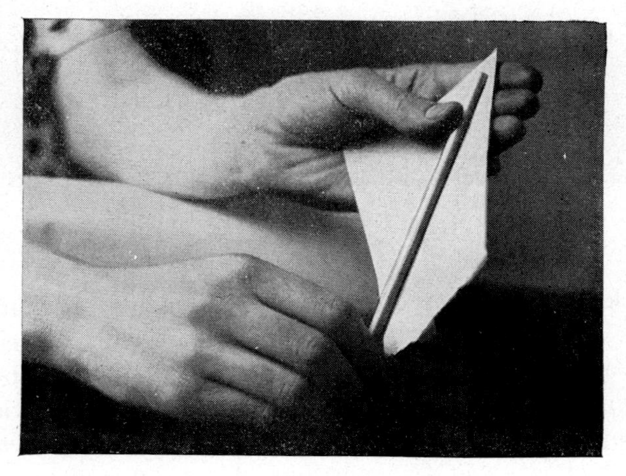

FIG. 91.
Sandpapering a Spar.

Now plane off the four corners, making the wood octagonal and finish by rasping or sandpapering, which will produce a straight and nicely tapered stick. Finish this by sandpapering as shown in fig. 91, holding the lower end of the stick in the right hand and resting it on a flat piece of sandpaper held in the left hand. Lightly pinch the stick between the left thumb and fingers and at the same time briskly rotate it and simultaneously move it upwards and downwards with the right hand. Prepare the upper masts in the same way, and then proceed with the yards and booms, which are similarly dealt with except that they taper from the middle towards each end. When completed, give them a coat of clear copal varnish as shown in fig. 92, supporting the end of

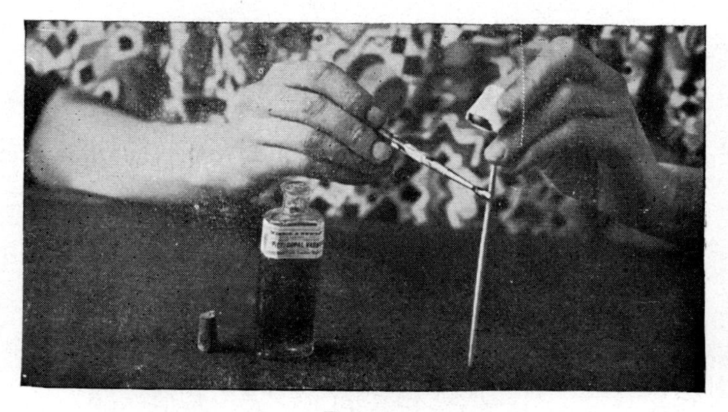

FIG. 92.
Varnishing the Spar.

the stick with a finger of the left hand while applying the varnish. A pin should be pressed into the end of the stick before varnishing it, and a cotton attached to the pin whereby to suspend the work from an overhead line while the varnish is drying. Now comes the construction of the various pieces which connect two portions of a mast and known as tops, caps, and crosstrees. Tops are roughly triangular in plan, and are attached to the lower masts, and to them the topmast shrouds are fastened, while the topmast itself rests in a square hole and is supported by another piece known as a fid. At the top of the lower mast is another part called the cap, represented in the model by a flat piece with two holes in it, one for the lower mast, the other for the topmast. Crosstrees and caps serve a similar purpose for the topmasts and topgallant masts. The words top, cap, and crosstrees are here used for convenience, although seamen and others will be aware that each consists in actual practice of several parts, each with its own particular name.

Now comes the question of how much detail is to be shown on these and other parts. Provided sufficient skill and patience, there is nothing to prevent the complete reproduction of every minute detail, but if each of these were only a very little over scale size the collective result would be greatly over size and appear ungainly; Moreover, the technical and manipulative skill needed for the work is of a very high order, consequently on the *Loch Torrens* a simplified construction has been adopted, which as can be seen from the numerous photographic illustrations leaves little to be desired and the work is well within the capabilities of the novice.

On the other hand, others may care to show much greater detail and for their benefit working drawings of many of the parts drawn to a larger scale are provided. These should be referred to for the overall dimensions of the parts, whether simplified or not, but the photographs of work in progress show what has to be done on the simplified system. Another general point to have in mind is that where references appear to the use of cardboard, it is usually just as practical to employ metal or wood of corresponding thickness, and in consequence when this is done a reference to adhesive for fastening wood or cardboard parts should be read as soldering or rivetting in the case of metals and *vice versa*. The author feels that the simplified methods will appeal to a wider circle of readers than a description of processes calling for greater technical skill and more properly the province of the professional.

Another general recommendation applying to all masting

and rigging is to separately fit each individual mast or spar, as although duplicates may appear identical in size, or be made apparently exactly to the drawings or dimensions, it will be found in practice that slight deviations have crept in and are sufficient to cause the parts to fit very indifferently.

The tops should be made by marking their shapes given in fig. 93 on stout card or thin wood about 1/16 in. thick, then

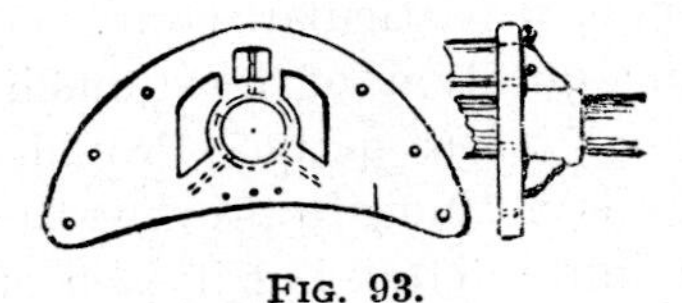

FIG. 93.
Detail of Tops.

drill or pierce all the holes and file them to shape where necessary, finally shape the exterior. If this procedure is reversed there is a risk of the material either splitting or being distorted. The holes can rapidly be pierced in cardboard with the square bradawl and with the same implement through thin metal.

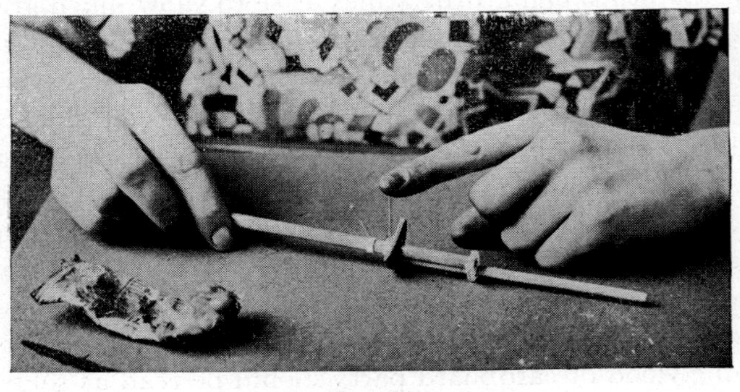

FIG. 94.
Fixing the Top.

The caps are made from card in a similar manner to the tops and when prepared should be fixed to the masts with adhesive, at the correct distance apart. Next cut some narrow strips of card and coil them around the mast, cut off sufficient to form a ring and fix this with adhesive to the mast, immediately below the top, and fix a similar ring a little below it, and to prevent the ends opening while the adhesive is drying, drive pins through them into the mast as shown in fig. 94, removing them as soon as the adhesive has set.

The caps for the topmasts are made in a different manner and are composed of separate narrow strips of card gummed around the masts. The cross-trees are cut to shape given in fig. 95 and attached to the masts with adhesive and fine pin points. The topgallant mast is then put into place, taking care to keep everything square and in line and bound to the topmast head by narrow strips of card, stuck in place as before. The two spreaders can be simply represented by stout pins driven into the mast and then cut to length.

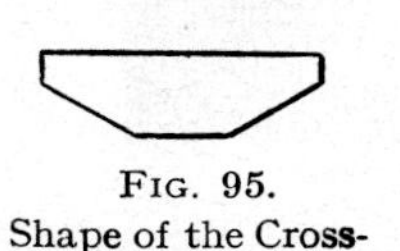

FIG. 95.
Shape of the Cross-trees.

FIG. 96.
Topmast with Spreaders Complete.

Small eyes are fixed to the after side of the cap, and to the underside of the topgallant mast as shown in fig. 96.

A considerable number of these eyes are required and are best made as necessary, from the pointed end of a fine pin, by bending them to shape with the snout-nosed pliers. The surplus is cut off and the eye then pressed into place as shown in fig. 97 with the small pliers.

These parts, and any other mast bands and similar pieces, should then be painted with eggshell black, or any other desired colour.

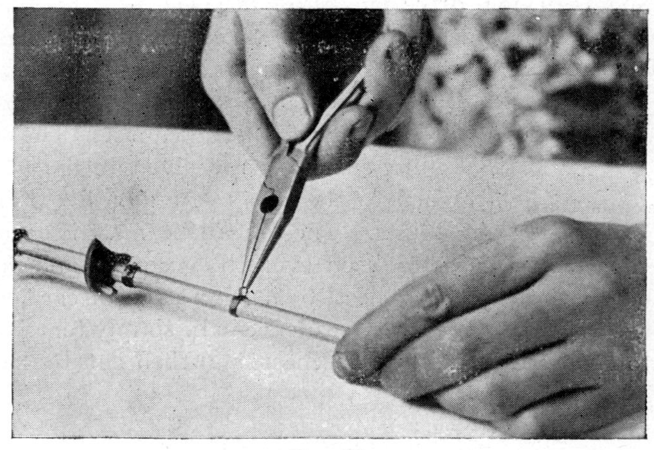

FIG. 97.
Fixing an Eye to the Mast.

The jigger mast on the *Loch Torrens* is composed of two pieces and united by a cap and crosstrees shown fully detailed in fig. 98 and simplified in fig. 99, which shows the parts assembled in place.

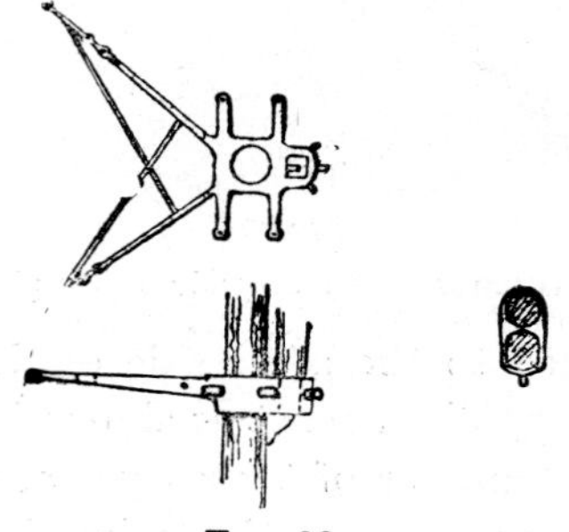

FIG. 98.
cap and Crosstrees for Jigger Mast.

The cap is similar to those for the other masts but the crosstrees are slightly different and are cut from card or thin wood in the same way as a top and similarly attached to the mast.

A vertical strip of metal known as a hank has to be fixed to the afterside of the lower jigger mast by means of two

FIG. 99.
Simplified Jigger Mast Assembled.

mast bands or hoops. The hank is a piece of 1/16 square sectioned tinned copper wire, reduced in thickness at each end to receive the hoops which may be of metal or card, the

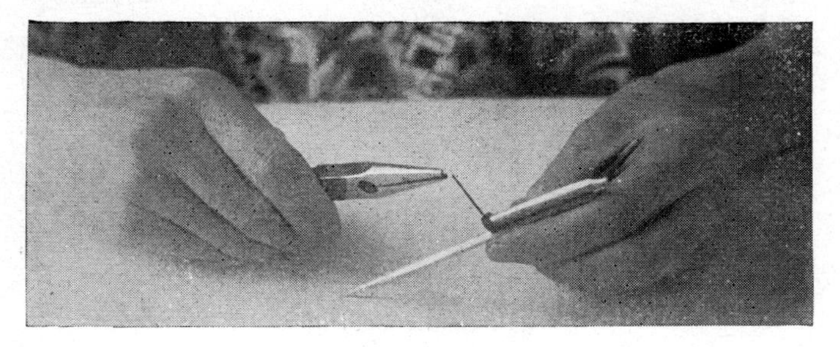

FIG. 100.
Fixing the Dolphin Striker.

latter proving satisfactory in practice for a model of this character.

The bowsprit and jibboom are made in a similar manner and are united by a cap having on the underside a pin with the head cut off as seen in fig. 100 to represent the dolphin striker and more fully detailed in fig. 101. The inboard end of the bowsprit is reduced in diameter and fits into a hole in the bows; it will be convenient to prepare it at this stage, but to fit it later on.

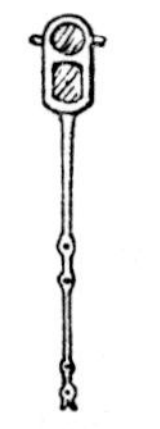

FIG. 101.
Detail of Bowsprit Cap.

There is no fixed order for the progress of the work, but it will be found convenient to prepare the yards and other spars next and to fit them with the requisite metal and other parts.

So far as the yards are concerned they are made and varnished in the same way as the masts, and may conveniently have the foot-ropes attached as soon as the varnish is quite hard.

FIG. 102.
Making the Footropes.

These are made of black cotton, and are spaced and arranged as shown on plate No. 4. The first operation is to tie short lengths to the spar to represent the stirrups, and a cotton is then tied to each yardarm at the extreme end to represent the footropes. Next steady the yard with pins as shown in fig. 102 to prevent movement and place other pins near the ends and the middle and at a little distance from the yard. Bring the cottons outside them and tie their free ends to the yard near to the centre, stretching them tightly between the pins, and then tie each stirrup to the footrope and secure them with a touch of adhesive, afterwards clipping off any surplus with a pair of very small scissors.

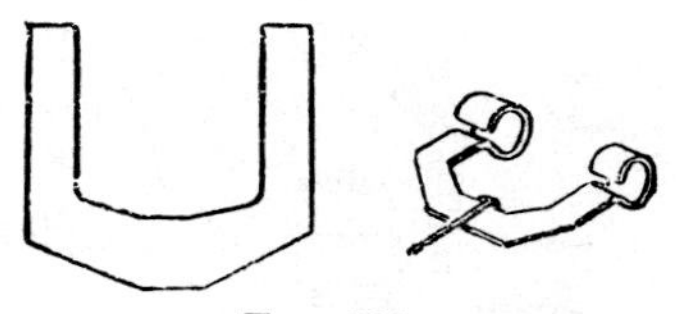

FIG. 103.
Lower Yard Truss.

The truss, or metal fittings by which the lower yards are attached to the masts have next to be made and the simplified pattern can be cut from sheet zinc to the shape shown in

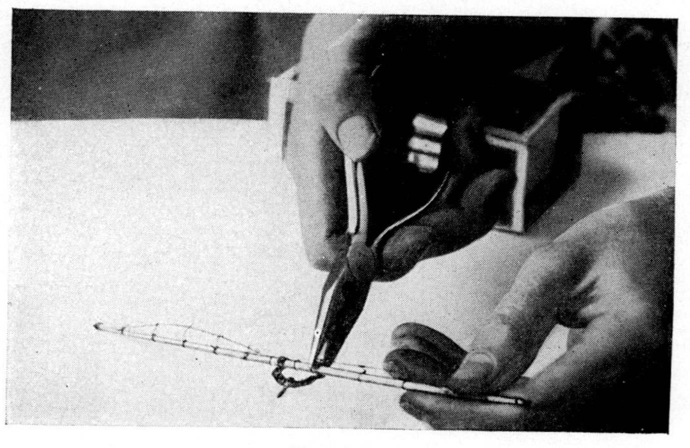

FIG. 104.
Fitting the Truss to the Yard.

fig. 103 using ordinary strong scissors. File the edges neatly, and then solder an ordinary pin to the middle part and paint it black. Then bend the ends to form eyes of a suitable diameter to grasp the yard; open them sufficiently and slip them on to the yard and close them again as shown in fig. 104 by gripping with the pliers.

The yard is then fastened to the mast by pushing the pin through the mast band (truss hoop) below the top, until the yard is in its place, cut off the surplus part of the pin,

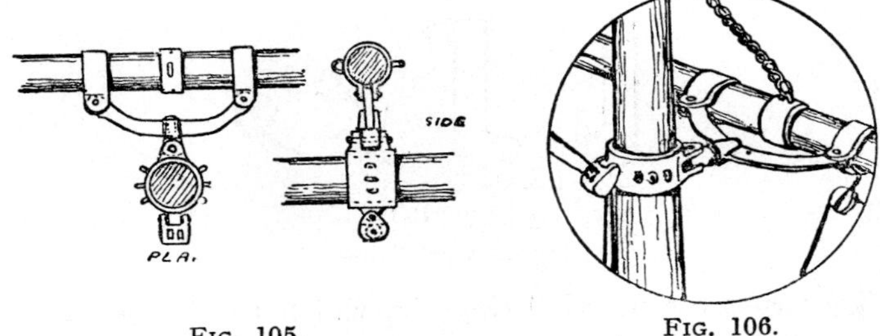

FIG. 105.
Fully Detailed Truss.

FIG. 106.
The Truss in Place.

and remove the yard, and set it aside until it is again needed. If a fully detailed truss is desired the requisite information can be had from figs. 105 and 106, the latter showing the completed truss in place together with some of the rigging. Treat all three lower yards in the same way and then make the

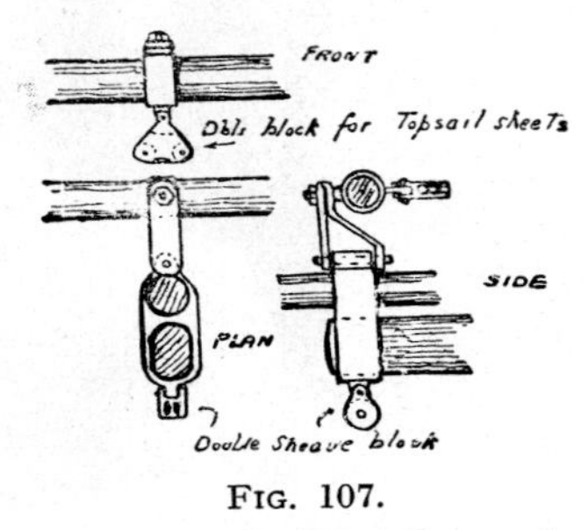

FIG. 107.
Lower Topsail Yard Ironwork.

brackets for the lower topsail yards, which are shown fully detailed in fig. 107. The simplified pattern is made by bending a narrow strip of sheet zinc to shape, and punching pin holes through the ends to form the bracket, which is then mounted on the foreside of the lower cap, by pressing a pin through it as shown in fig. 108 and nipping off the surplus. The yard is then attached to the bracket as shown in fig. 109 by passing a pin through it and the yard until the pin head

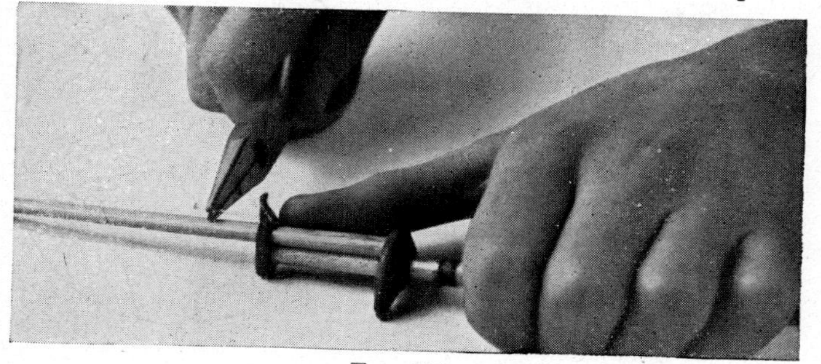

Fig. 108.
Fitting the Lower Topsail Yard Bracket.

Fig. 109.
Fitting the Yard to the Bracket.

bears on the bracket and subsequently turning the lower part of the pin to form a small eye from which to suspend the double sheet block, as described on page 178, Chapter XIII.

The upper topsail yard has to be arranged so that it can be raised or lowered on the mast, and the fully detailed fitting is illustrated in figs. 110 and 111, but the simplified

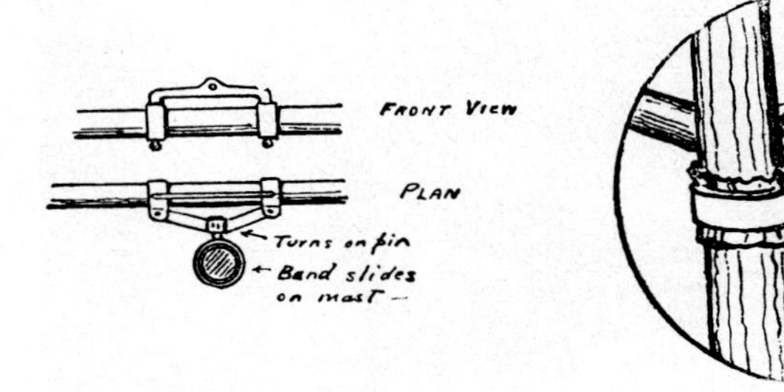

FIG. 110
Fully detailed Upper Topsail Yard Ironwork.

FIG. 111.
Upper Topsail Yard Ironwork Fitted.

pattern for the *Loch Torrens* is shown in fig. 112. This is simply a ring made of sheet zinc, with a pin passed through it and bent over to form an eye. Another pin is bent to form the yardiron, and the two soldered together as shown

FIG. 112.
Making Simple Upper Topsail Yard Ironwork.

in fig. 112, which also shows how the pieces are held steadily by other pins while the soldering operations are in progress. Little strips of thin card are then gummed to the yards and after the fittings have been painted they are pressed through these bands and into the yard at right angles to the footrope and jackstay as is clearly visible in fig. 113, which also shows the halyard strap, similarly made from a pin and pressed into the upper part of the yard.

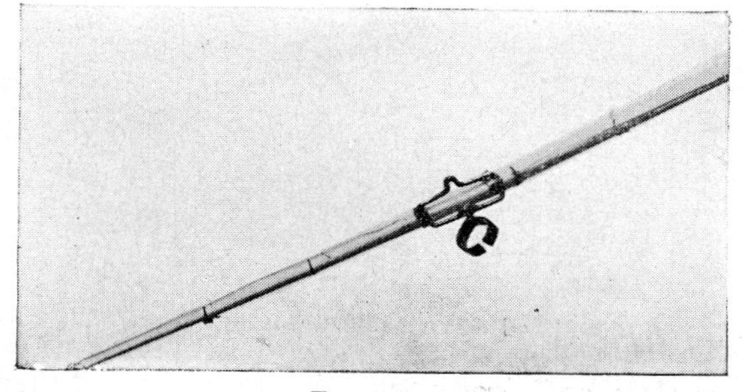

FIG. 113.
Upper Topsail Ironwork Fitted to the Yard.

The topgallant and royal yards are held to the mast by parrels, or loops of stout thread or soft copper wire, as is clearly seen in figs. 114 and 115, the latter showing the simplified form for the *Loch Torrens*, which is quickly made from No. 22 gauge soft copper wire, twisted around the yard, with an eye to surround the mast.

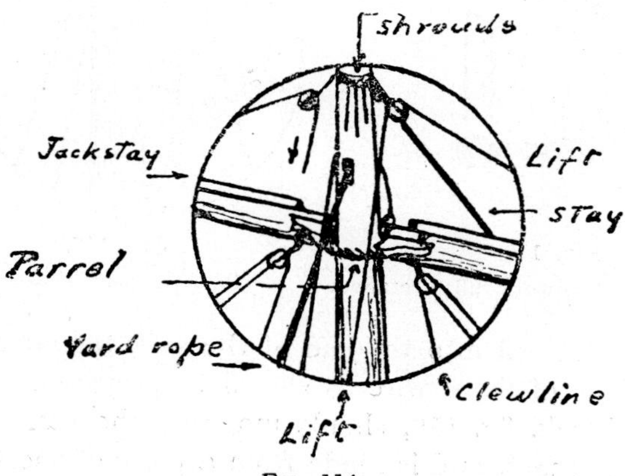

FIG. 114.
Details of Parrel Fitted to the Yard.

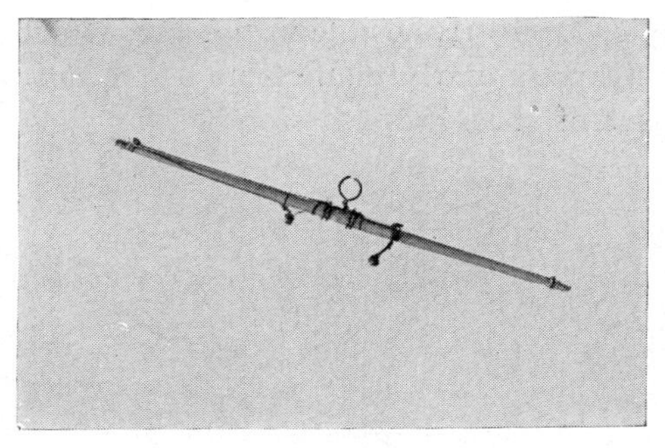

FIG. 115.
Simplified Parrel Fitted to the Yard.

The spanker gaff ironwork, shown fully detailed in fig. 116 and fitted in fig. 117, is an intricate piece of work, but the simple form shown in fig. 118 consists of a pin bent to

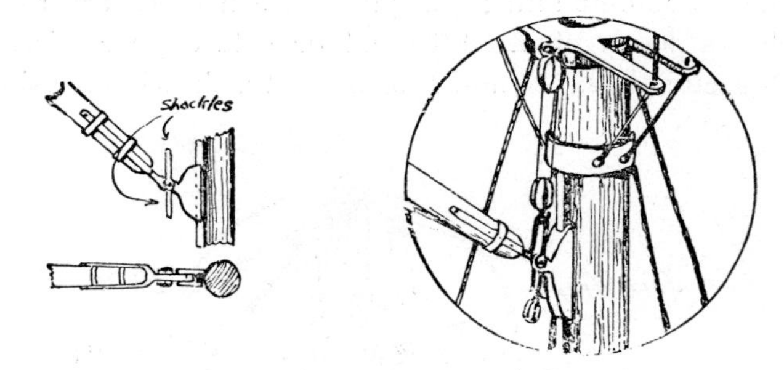

FIG. 116.
Spanker Gaff Ironwork fully Detailed.

FIG. 117.
Spanker Gaff Fitted.

shape and pressed into the end of the gaff, the latter having two bindings of floral wire as shown to prevent it splitting. The slide block, fig. 119, should move on the hank or metal strip on the mast, and is made from a piece of sheet zinc by cutting and filing it to shape and then bending it in the middle, and the eye on the end of the pin closed around it, all these parts being shown in the diagram (fig. 118). The boom ironwork in detail is given in figs. 120 and 121 and simplified in fig. 118, the latter consisting of a narrow strip of zinc driven into a slot in the end of the boom, and secured by two bindings of floral wire. The end of the strip fits into the jaws of a small "U" sectioned piece or jaw and is hinged to it by a

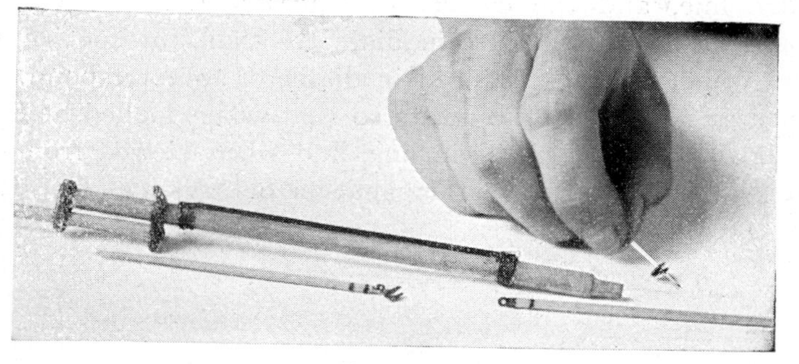

FIG. 118.
Simplified Ironwork for Spanker Gaff.

small rivet made from a pin. The jaws are free to turn on a small staple bent to shape from a pin and driven into the lower mast hoop as shown in fig. 118. The spenser gaff,

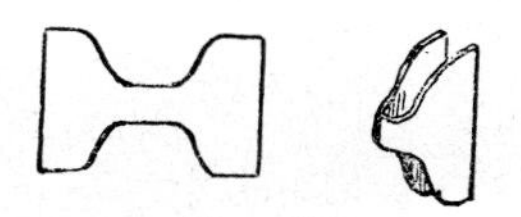

FIG. 119.
Detail of Slide Block.

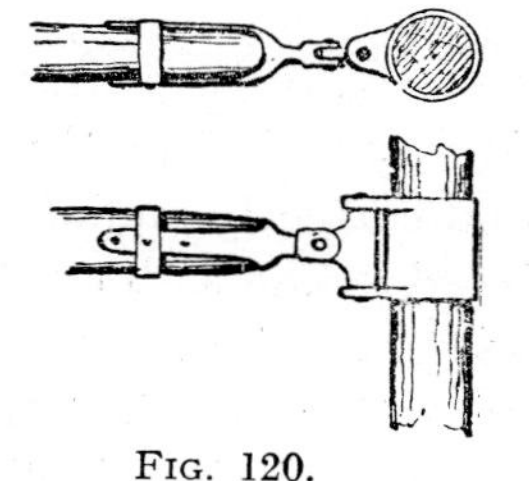

FIG. 120.
Spanker Boom Ironwork.

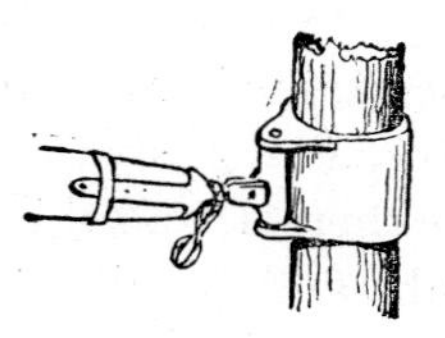

FIG. 121.
Spanker Boom Fitted.

if fitted, should be similarly dealt with or may be provided with a simple gaff jaw.

This completes the constructional work on the masts

and spars, and the masts can now be set up or "stepped" on the hull. In the case of the *Loch Torrens* or any other model with a solid hull, holes have to be bored into the deck on the centre line, and the correct distances apart. These holes should be a little smaller in diameter than the foot of the mast which must be reduced in diameter to correspond. It is necessary to step the masts so that when looked at from the bows they will all be in line, and when viewed from the side will have the correct inclination or "rake." The rake

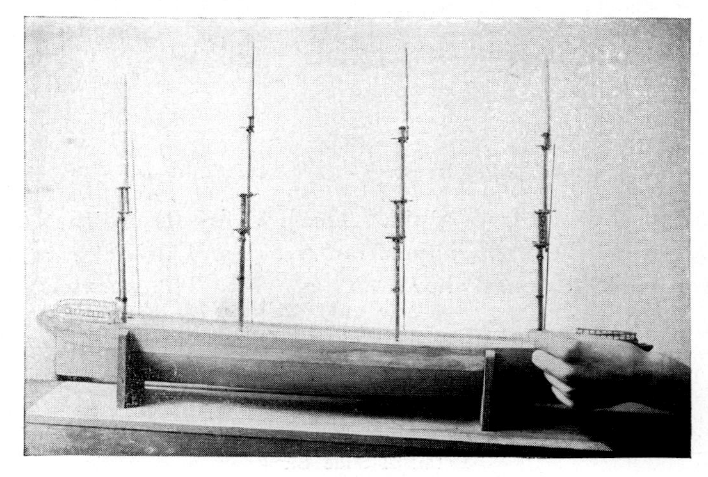

FIG. 122.
Adjusting Rake of Masts.

can be ascertained from the drawings, and if four thick lines be drawn on a large sheet of card and correctly inclined to the lower edge thereof, and this edge placed in line with the L.W.L. on the hull, and parallel to the latter, as shown in fig. 122, to guide the eye it becomes an easy matter to adjust the ends (heel) of the masts until they have a similar inclination. The masts should not now be fixed permanently, as much of the standing rigging and some of the running rigging has to be completed and added as described in subsequent chapters.

CHAPTER X.

DECK FITTINGS.

Similarly Detailed Treatment of Deck Fittings, Including How to Make Them, and How to Fix Them, and in What Order—Fully Illustrated with Line Drawings and Photographs.

The term deck fittings is used in model shipbuilding to describe the numerous erections, davits, anchors and other gear which is usually found on deck. The construction of such parts is very interesting, and any desired amount of detail can be represented according to personal taste and ability. The commercially made exhibition fittings require most delicate work, and an absolutely faithful adherence to scale and proportion, as they are subjected to the most discriminating criticism when displayed in a public museum. Their construction calls for exceptional ability and patience, acquired only by long experience and apprenticeship to a practical firm of ship modellers.

On the other hand, the making of practical fittings for a model like the *Loch Torrens* is not such a formidable undertaking, as provided the character is retained all merely superfluous detail can be omitted. As it is impracticable to give detailed drawings of all deck fittings used on the many different types and periods of clipper ships, the following alphabetically arranged description of those which may be termed "standard" has been prepared in the confident anticipation it would be of general utility.

Specific details of construction are not given for each with the exception of representative examples for use on *Loch Torrens*. Most of the smaller fittings are preferably made from metal, chiefly wire of various sections, thin sheet or strip brass and zinc.

The principal requisites for making any high grade fittings are a small accurate lathe, hand tools, small blow-pipe, and above all care and patience. The metal used to the exclusion of practically any other is brass, while the finish is generally silver or gold plating, bronzing, oxydising, and lacquering in colour completed by a coat of clear lacquer. A number of fittings can be purchased ready for use, at

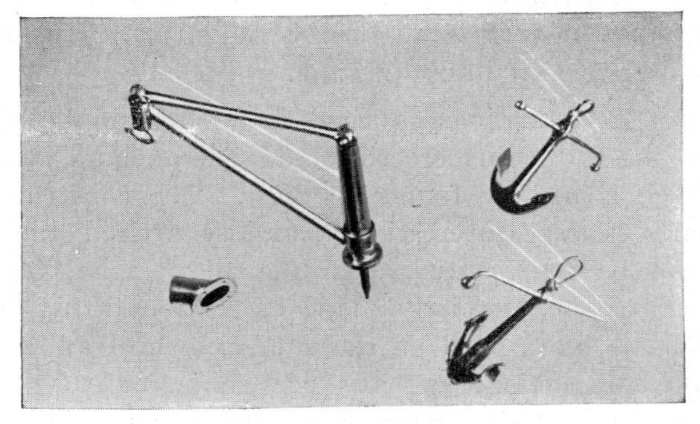

FIG. 123.
(Top) Anchor Crane. Roger's Anchor.
(Bottom) Chain Lead. Trotman's Anchor.

moderate prices, but it is essential to select only those with the proper character and size.

On *Loch Torrens* the whole of the fittings are hand made from simple materials and the result is tolerably good as can be judged by the numerous photographic illustrations, and the novice need have no hesitation in adopting these simplified methods of construction.

An Accommodation Ladder is a hanging staircase suspended from small davits on the ship's side, provided with wooden treads or stairs, and a landing platform at top and bottom, usually in the form of a grating, with stanchions and hand-rail.

Anchor.—Various types are in use, one of the principal patterns as shown in fig. 123 is known as a "Trotman's" anchor, and is extensively used on clipper ships. The Roger's anchor is more appropriate for early clippers or small craft. The cross-bar is detachable, making stowage on deck comparatively simple. The anchors on *Loch Torrens* are sawn and filed to shape from sheet ebonite, about 1/8 in. thick, and fitted with a wire cross-bar and shackle as shown

FIG. 124.
Forecastle of *Loch Torrens.*

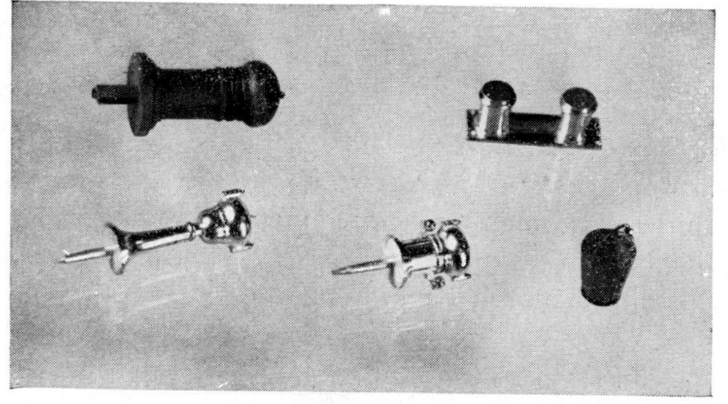

FIG. 125.
(Top) Wooden Binnacle. Bollards.
(Bottom) Plain Binnacle. Thomson's Binnacle. Fire Bucket.

in fig. 124 in place on the forecastle. The ebonite can be cut quite easily with a fretsaw or any fine-toothed hand saw, and is drilled or filed like any ordinary hard wood or metal and polished with emery paper.

Binnacles.—These are sometimes known as compass stands,

and are of various types, the plain simple patterns shown in fig. 125, and the improved and patented pattern known as the "Thomson's." That used on *Loch Torrens* was made with plastic wood, filed to shape when hard and then painted.

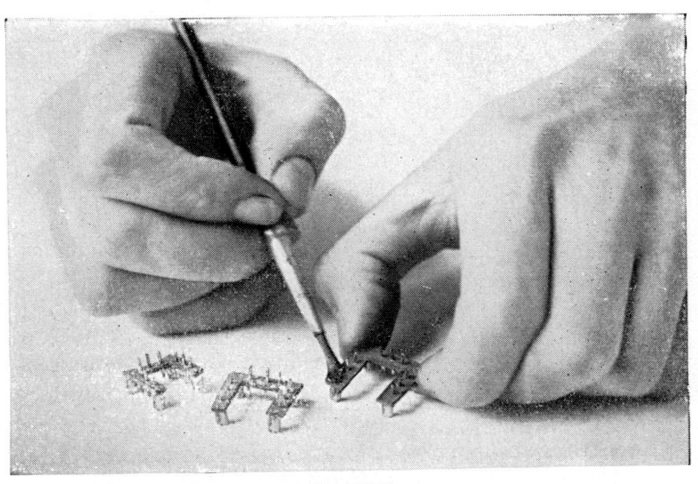

FIG. 126.
Making the Bitts and Pin Rail.

Bitts and Pin Rails.—The masts are usually surrounded with a wooden structure known as the bitts, and are provided with pin rails; such an arrangement is shown in fig. 126, in simplified form as used on *Loch Torrens,* and made from card, pins and match stick.

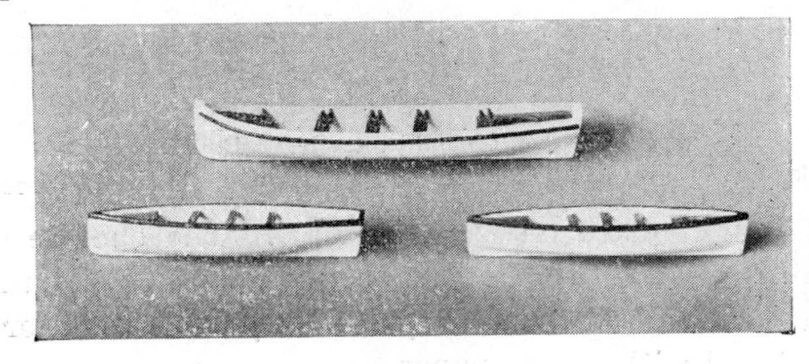

FIG. 127.
Ships' Boats.

Boats.—Ships' boats are many and various in design, but, broadly speaking for model work, are of three types—

(*a*) Open boats with transom stern as in fig. 127.

(*b*) Open boats of the "lifeboat" type with both ends pointed.

(*c*) Covered boats as used on ocean-going vessels when at sea. These are of course only the ordinary open ships' boats, but protected by a canvas covering.

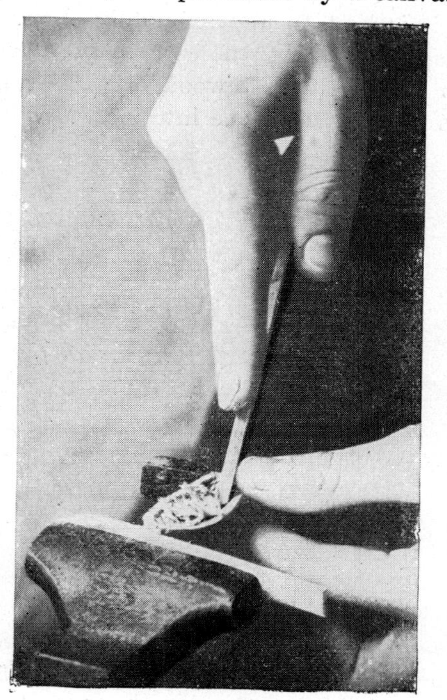

Fig. 128.

Carving a Ship's Boat.

The open boats may be quite simple in construction, and carved from pine, with two or three cross pieces of thin card to represent the thwarts or seats as was done for the *Loch Torrens*; on larger models they may be elaborately finished with knees, treads and oars, as at the top of fig. 127.

The covered boats are very easily made, and generally left solid. The proportions of the boats do not vary with variations of the scale, consequently by following the shapes shown on the folding plate No. 5 a serviceable and accurate boat will be obtained. Dinghys are, however, generally rather broader and deeper, while gigs are slightly narrower in proportion to the length. Any of the simple types of ships' boats can be carved from the solid in the same way as the hull; it is best to approximately shape the exterior, and then grasp the boat by the ends in the vice as shown in fig. 128 with some felt, soft wood or similar material over the vice jaws while carving the interior.

FIG. 129.
Mast Bands. Shackle. Turnbuckle. Deadeye. Cleat.

Bollards.—Are used for mooring purposes to make fast the hawsers which hold the vessel to the quayside. They are easily made, and may with advantage be freely used in their proper places on the model. Fig. 125 is the usual pattern, and for the *Loch Torrens* (fig. 141) is made from a narrow strip of card, with two tiny pieces of shaped match stick gummed to the upper side, and the whole painted black and then gummed in place on the deck.

Boom and Mast Fittings.—The many derricks and booms used on shipboard necessitate considerable rigging, and to facilitate this some amount of metal work is required, that most generally used being a metal band with four eyes, as shown in fig. 129. These are supplied as stock fittings in all sizes from 3/16 in. to 1 in. diameter, either with eyes or with belaying pins.

Cable or Anchor Chain is obtainable in a variety of styles, the simplest being the common round link, bent to shape from thin wire; an improvement is to solder the ends of each link together, while the best and proper anchor cable should be studded, that is, should have a little cross bar soldered in place across each link.

Cabins and Deck Erections generally are usually made from blocks of evenly grained wood and hand-painted, or are built up from narrow strips. On a model as small as the *Loch Torrens* they are most readily constructed from 3-ply Bristol board, and when neatly painted with water colours present an attractive appearance; a group of the fittings for the *Loch Torrens* is shown in fig. 130 made in this way. The

FIG. 130.
Group of Deck Erections for *Loch Torrens.*

method is to set out on a strip of card the elevation of all four sides of the cabin, and the windows and doors neatly drawn from the details given on plate No. 5. Include a tab at one end for fastening purposes, score the corners and bend the strip as shown in fig. 131, and gum the tab end to the inside of the other end. Add a flat roof made from card, sticking this in place with seccotine, and then paint the windows, doors and the like. This class of fitting can be made to seat accurately on a cambered deck by placing a smooth piece of fine sandpaper flat on the deck and gently

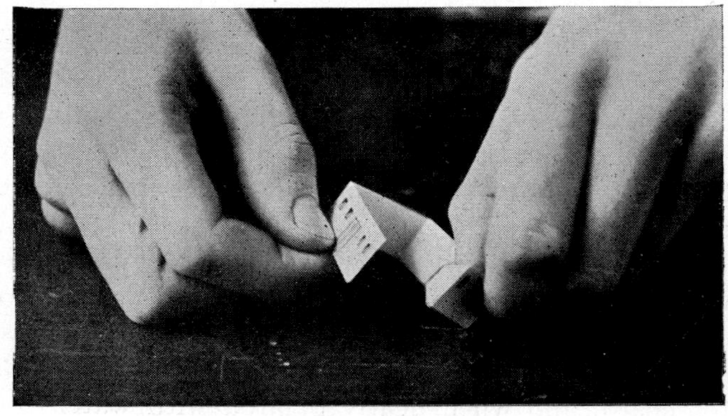

FIG. 131.
Shaping a Cabin.

pushing the fitting backwards and forwards along it as shown in fig. 132 until the lower edges are sufficiently curved, after which it can be gummed in place. Other fittings which can

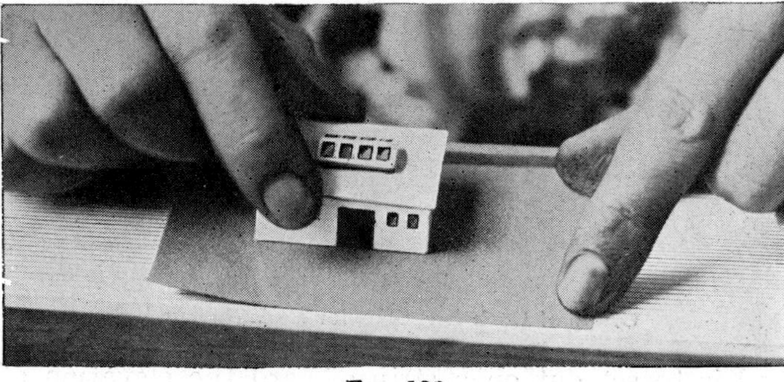

FIG. 132.
Cambering the Underside of a Cabin.

be made in the same way are deck seats, skylights, hatch covers and the like. In cases such as *Loch Torrens*, where the poop and forecastle bulkheads are formed from the solid, it is desirable to face them as shown in fig. 133 with 3-ply Bristol board neatly lined out and painted in appropriate colours.

FIG. 133.
Bulkhead Card Fitted to the Poop.

Capstans are used to hoist in an anchor by winding in the cable, or to lift heavy weights, warp a boat alongside a wharf, and so forth. There are many patterns, but fig. 134 shows

FIG. 134.
Capstans, Steam and Hand.

the commercially-made merchant service type, as used on sailing vessels, while on larger craft a steam capstan such as shown is sometimes employed. The capstans on *Loch Torrens* are very small and can be made as shown in fig. 135 by grasping a small piece of hard wood in the chuck of the hand drill, rotating the latter with one hand while manipulating a piece of sandpaper with the other. The hand drill is gripped in the vice and thus acts in some measure as a small turning lathe, and many other small parts can be made in the same way. Chain leads and chain pipes (fig. 123) are used to convey the cable from the chain lockers in the forepeak, to

FIG. 135.
Shaping a Capstan for *Loch Torrens*.

the capstan and thence to the anchors; they are usually made from a small piece of brass tube with a flange at the end.

Cleats (fig. 129), used to make fast a sheet or running rope, are made from card, boxwood or ebonite and pinned in place.

Companions are used for access from one deck to another.

Fig. 136.
Companion, made of Mahogany.

They are usually made of thin wood or cardboard and fig. 136 gives an excellent idea of the appearance.

Cowls, sometimes called ventilators, are provided to

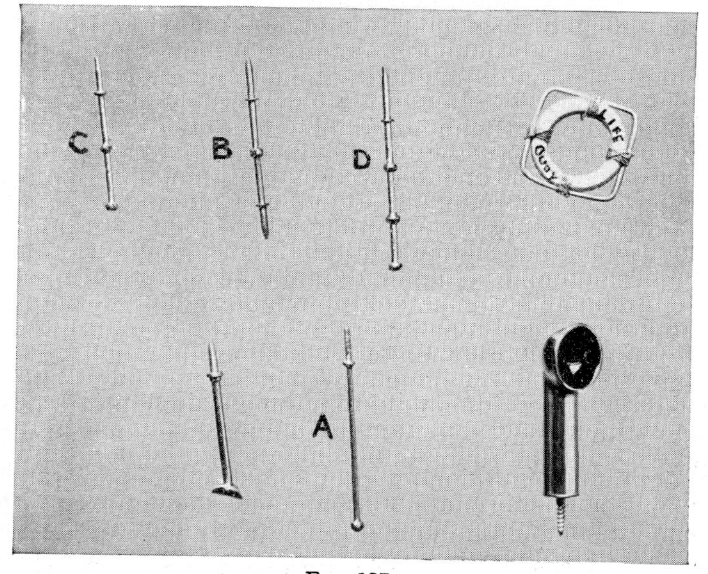

Fig. 137.
(Top) 3 Stanchions. Lifebuoy.
(Bottom) Galley Funnel. Single Rail Stanchion. Cowl.

admit air to the interior of a vessel; usually the expression is confined to the smaller sizes of ventilators. A commercial design is shown in fig. 137, and is made from metal. The small vents on the *Loch Torrens* are modelled in plastic wood, finished by sandpapering and neatly painted black on the exterior and red in the bowl.

Davits are used chiefly for hoisting in the ships' boats, and raising the anchors. Fig. 138 shows two types of single

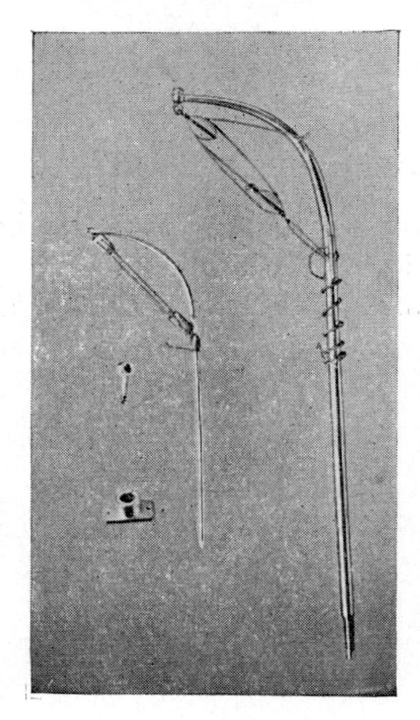

FIG. 138.
Ship's Davits and Sockets.

arm davit. Simplified davits of the regulation pattern can be made from brass wire nicely bent to shape, and drilled at the top to take the upper block. A more detailed fitting has a proper tapering arm with ball and chain plate at the top and belaying pin or cleat near by at the bottom. Davits are fitted to the hull in various ways; those on the ship's side can have a deck or rail plate, and a socket as shown.

The plates can be constructed from thin sheet metal and

the davits turned from brass rod. The blocks and tackle can be purchased for a few pence ready made, although if desired the blocks can be shaped from pieces of boxwood.

FIG. 139.
Fixing Boat Skids

FIG. 140.
Davits in Place.

In the case of boats stowed on an upper deck a rail plate is used on the bulwark top rail and a footstep or base plate on the lower deck. When rail or deck plates are not convenient side sockets (fig. 138) can be used in their stead. Three of the boats on *Loch Torrens* are stowed on skids (fig. 139), spanning the ship and passing over the roof of the forward cabin. These skids are shaped from 4-ply Bristol board, with webs of 2-ply board, or could be represented by wires bent to shape. On larger models they are best made from strip or sheet brass soldered at all joints. In each case they have chocks for stowage of the boats and eye-bolts for the lashings. The davits for the *Loch Torrens* are clearly shown in fig. 140. Fitted in place by inserting them into holes drilled in the deck.

Deck Tubs and Buckets are generally provided as an aid in extinguishing fire, and also for use when swabbing the decks; the fire bucket is shown in fig. 125 and they are simply made of hard wood or from card and match stick (fig. 141), showing a typical bucket rack as used for the *Loch Torrens.*

Eye-plates are used for attaching the standing end of rigging and consist of a flat base plate of metal with a wire eye-bolt securely attached, while on *Loch Torrens* they are represented by card and a bent pin as in fig. 141.

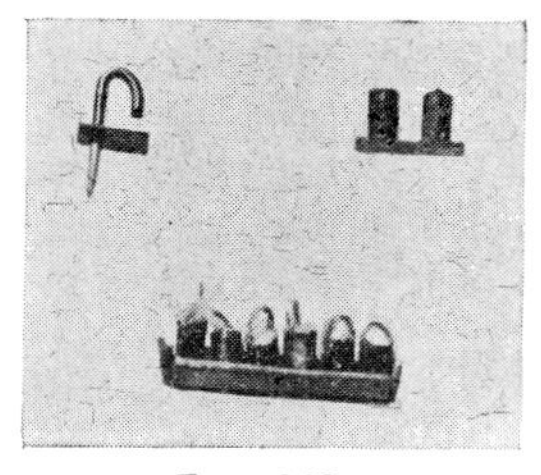

FIG. 141.
(Top) Eye-plate and Bollard.
(Bottom) Bucket Rack for *Loch Torrens.*

Fairleads are devices to guide a rope without chafing over the ship's side. The mercantile patterns are generally plain, as in fig. 142, while another pattern is frequently used on large vessels, the central vertical pulley reducing the friction on the hawsers. Smaller patterns are used for guiding the headsail sheets on the forecastle. The fairleads for ***Loch Torrens*** are shown in fig. **124**, and shaped from card.

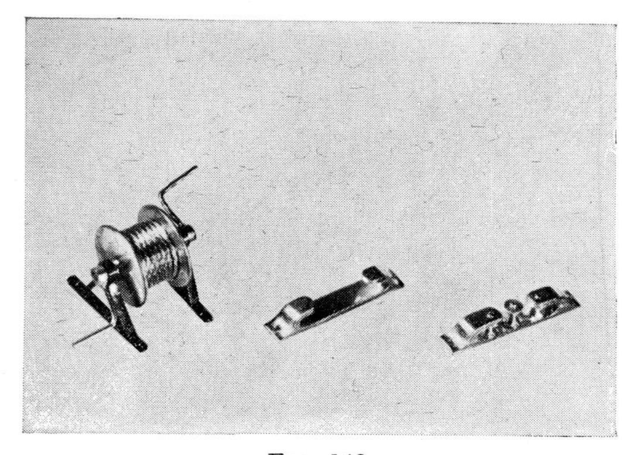

FIG. 142.
Hawser Reel and Fairleads.

Hawse Pipes are provided at the bows of a vessel to guide the anchor cable. They are usually made of brass tube and the method of fixing is to mark off their upper position on the deck, and to mark the lower position on the outside of the hull, and then to drill small holes from these points in a straight line until they meet, afterwards enlarging the hole until the tube can be passed straight through when the

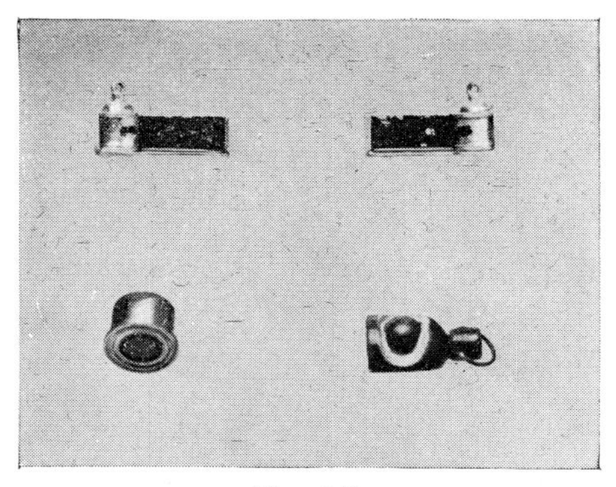

Fig. 143.
Head, Side and Dead Lights.

projecting ends should be filed almost flush with the deck and the ship's side, and a half-round ring fitted at each side of the tube.

Headlights (fig. 143) are used at the masthead to show a white riding light, and can be made from tube, or modelled in plastic wood.

FIG. 144.
Ship Ladders.

Ladders.—Two types (fig. 144) are in general use on shipboard—(*a*) Those with round rungs and made entirely in metal, generally called a Jacob's ladder; (*b*) Ladders having flat treads and made of wood, a more elaborate ladder becoming a staircase. Ladders are always difficult things to make on very small models. One method, used on *Loch Torrens*, is to drive pins at regular intervals through a piece of card of the desired width then clip off the ends and file them perfectly level. Next solder to them the side pieces which may be 1/16 square tinned copper wire. When the soldering is complete, the sides are carefully reduced in thickness, and the card then cut away, the result being a very effective and neat ladder. The other pattern can be made with card in a similar way by cutting slits in the edge of a piece of card, loading them with tiny treads made from card and then gumming the sides to their ends.

Lifebuoys (fig. 137) are for use in saving life, when a person falls overboard, and can be represented by a ring of card or bone.

Pin Rail, a long shelf or board fixed about one-third of the way down the bulwarks from the top, to receive belaying pins which fit into holes in the rail. The belaying pins can be neatly turned to shape from brass wire, or more simply represented by pins, driven into the bulwark side.

FIG. 145.
Pumps—Main, Forecastle and Downton.

Pumps are important fittings on a clipper ship. The Downton pump (fig. 145) is available ready made but its construction is simple, and readily effected from brass rod and wire. The two other patterns of pumps are shown in detail on plate No. 5 for the *Loch Torrens*; the forecastle pump, (fig. 145) is made from wood, zinc and pins; the main pumps (fig. 145) are almost entirely of wire. The hand wheels are wire rings with spokes soldered to them and the whole soldered to a shaft made from wire bent to shape and the whole then mounted on the bitts around the main and mizen masts

Purchase Reel (fig. 142), a form of small crab or winch, used for soundings and light haulage and lifting purposes on deck.

Shackles (fig. 129).—Connect the ends of a cable to an anchor, or are used for other similar purposes.

Sidelights (fig. 143) are used to enable other mariners to know at night in which direction a vessel is proceeding. The starboard, or right-hand side of a boat looking from the stern forwards, is always green, and the left-hand or port side always red. The masthead light is always white. The side lights are generally carried in a boxlike structure as shown in fig. 143, which is a good all-round pattern for general use.

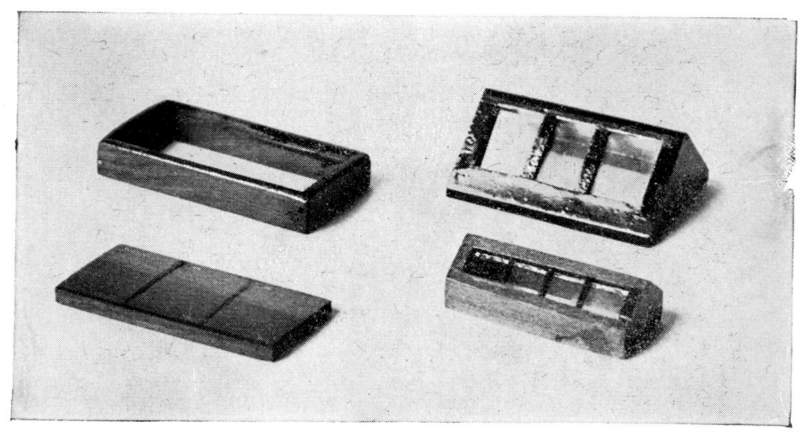

FIG. 146.
Skylight and Hatch Cover.

Those on the *Loch Torrens* are made from card and the lamps from a match stick, but on larger models should be entirely of metal.

Skylights, as the name implies, are provided on deck to admit light to the spaces beneath. For a model the simple pattern (fig. 146) is quite good enough, but a more elaborate fitting is shown in plate No. 5 combined with eating accommodation.

Stanchions are very numerous. Various standard patterns are shown in fig. 137: (*a*) Being for a single rail only, (*b*) for single metal rail and wood toprail, (*c*) for two rails, and (*d*) for three rails. Their use on a deck side to prevent passengers falling overboard is obvious. Stanchions are very difficult things to model, and it is preferable to buy them, but for

FIG. 147.
Making the Forecastle Rail.

clipper ships of the size and character of *Loch Torrens* the commercial patterns are too big, and a tolerable substitute is to make them in the following way. First drive pins into the deck at the desired spacing, and then clip off the surplus. Next bend a piece of 1/16 square tinned copper wire to the exact shape and lay it on top of the row of pins, drive down any of them which are too high, and until all are level at the tops. Then interlace the pins with a length of floral wire, placed about midway of the pins, fastening one end to any convenient external spot, and after drawing the wire taut fasten the other end in a similar way. Then solder the toprail and the floral wire, as shown in fig. 147, clip off any surplus wire and paint the toprail brown and the other parts white.

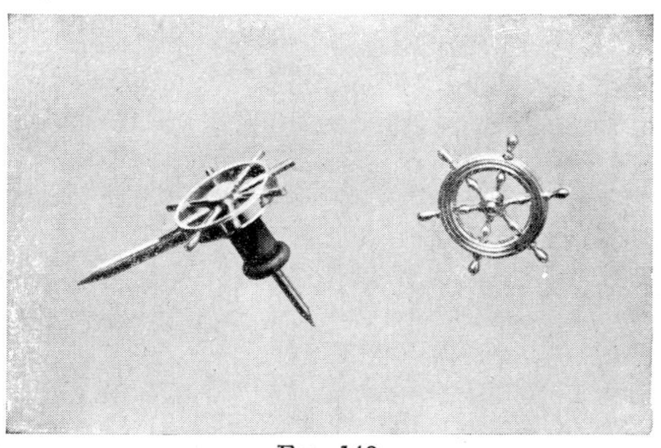

FIG. 148.
Steering Wheels.

FIG. 149.
Steering Wheel and Case for *Loch Torrens* Compared with a Coin.

Steering Wheels are used to operate the rudder, through suitable gear and tackle; fig. 148 shows the general types of wheel employed on a model clipper ship.

Their construction to a very small scale is a difficult

matter, it can be done with thin wire, patience and a soldering iron, but a splendid substitute is to cut a disc from a piece of thin clear celluloid and to outline on it in black, the rim, spokes and handles, and then mount it on a pin on the steering gear case which can be made as before described, from thin Bristol board. This was done on the *Loch Torrens*, and fig. 149 shows how effective it is, especially when compared in size with the adjacent coin.

Turnbuckles, sometimes called strainers, are useful on large models for setting up rigging, and a typical pattern is shown in fig. 129; they are troublesome to make and consequently are preferably purchased ready for use.

Winch.—Used for handling heavy loads and dealing with topsail sheets and the like. The pattern used on *Loch Torrens* is detailed in plate No. 5 and shown finished in fig. 150, and is made from sheet zinc, pins and Bristol board for the gear wheels, with wooden drums.

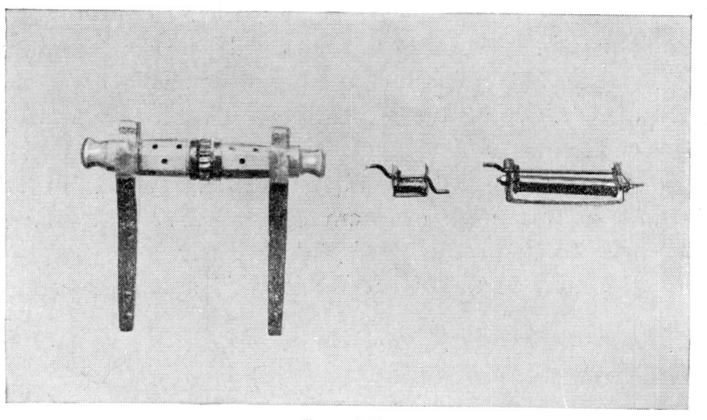

FIG. 150.
Early Windlass, Winch and Windlass.

Windlass.—Various patterns have been used on clippers; an early windlass in shown in fig. 150, that on the *Loch Torrens* is fairly typical, the working drawings are given in plate No. 5 and a view of the finished article in fig. 150.

They are made with sheet zinc side frames, wooden drums and pins for the axles and handles, the gear wheels are made from cardboard.

The discs for the gears are first cut to approximate size and shape, then mounted on a peg and revolved in the hand-drill, and sandpapered to a circular form; the teeth are then represented by holding a new coin against the edge of the card while the latter is revolving and allowing the coin to rotate between the fingers and thumb, which speedily indents the edge of the card and gives a good representation of the gear teeth.

All deck fittings should be prepared before the standing and running rigging is set up, and may be permanently fixed in place at any convenient time according to their position or purpose.

Generally speaking, it is best to fix them at a fairly early stage, say when the standing rigging has been set up, but before dealing with running rigging and the sails. The hull should of course be painted before the masts and gear are permanently fixed, but the last coat of enamel, polish or varnish can be applied after all the other work is completed.

There are other deck fittings that could be modelled, including such things as the ship's bell, hencoops, deck lights, seats and so forth; all of them can, however, be made on similar lines to the above, and added or not according to the style of the model and the inclination of the modeller.

CHAPTER XI.

THE STANDING RIGGING.

THE FOLDING PLATE SHOWS ALL THE STANDING RIGGING IN POSITION AND DETAILS OF EVERY STAGE AND PROCESS OF THE WORK ARE GIVEN—WELL ILLUSTRATED BY NUMEROUS LINE DRAWINGS, AND PHOTOGRAPHS.

THE standing rigging of a model clipper ship, as indeed of any ship, comprises all those fixed ropes or wires which support the masts and bowsprit. It consists chiefly of the shrouds, which support a mast in a transverse or athwartships direction, and stays which perform a similar duty in a fore and aft direction.

To adequately steady and secure a mast or spar it must have at least three separate supports, arranged in a triangular manner when seen in plan. For example, a stay to support a mast from some forward position, and a shroud on each side of the mast to some point on deck or in the hull side, and a little behind, or aft, of the mast fulfils these conditions. The shrouds are, however, multiplied as one alone would be inadequate, and in practice the mast is further supported by backstays, which are ropes going from the head of any upper mast to the sides of the ship, at a point somewhat aft of the mast.

Other ropes which perform analogous duties for specific spars are named as follows:—*Guys*, the side supports of a boom. The bowsprit is supported downwards by *bobstays* and sideways by *shrouds*, the jibboom is supported downwards by a martingale and sideways by *jib-guys*, the flying jibboom downwards by a *flying martingale* and sideways by *flying guys*. In passing it should be noted that on relatively early clippers the foregoing were generally adopted, but on more recent ships the tendency to simplification is more pronounced and in some cases a single piece bowsprit with rigid iron guys and bobstay does duty for the former arrangements.

Also on earlier clippers, *gaffs* were used to spread the rigging of the jib and flying jibbooms, and a *dolphin striker* in connection with the martingale, while whiskers or sprit-sail gaffs were employed in connection with the jib-guys.

The novice looking at a well-rigged model such as the *Cutty Sark* (fig. 151), made with great fidelity by Bassett-Lowke Ltd., may feel a little confused by the seeming complexity of the ropes and be bothered by their proper denomination. Fortunately every guy, stay, shroud and backstay has the same name as the spar which it supports, thus, for example, those supporting a fore topmast are called fore topmast stay, fore topmast shrouds, fore topmast backstays, and similarly with all the others.

As all these ropes are fixtures (or sufficiently so for the purpose of the ship modeller), it follows that they have to be firmly attached at each end and that some means be provided to tighten them. On early ships the universal way of tightening the shrouds was by means of *dead-eyes* and a lanyard. Dead-eyes were usually circular pieces of wood and had three holes through them, and a groove around the edge, the latter to receive the shroud which was taken around the dead-eye, and the end turned inwards around the shroud. A second dead-eye was similarly stropped and shackled or otherwise attached to the chain plates. The lanyard, a thinner rope, was then passed through the holes drawn tight and secured. For model work the shroud can be seized around the dead-eye, and the lanyard rove through as above, the whole as shown in fig. 152. On later ships an iron dead-eye was used, and in more recent times a rigging screw (fig. 129) or turnbuckle, the

FIG. 151.

Scale Model of *Cutty Sark*.

shroud then turned in round a heart-shaped thimble attached to the rigging screw.

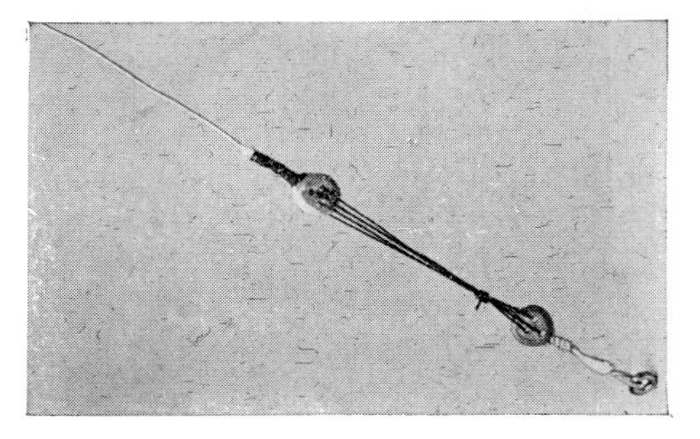

FIG. 152.

Dead-eyes and Lanyard.

The upper or standing end of a single stay is usually fitted with an eye-splice, around the mast, and pairs of stays, by a bight secured with a seizing. Shrouds are generally fitted in pairs, with a throat seizing on the bight, around the masthead, the foremost pair on the starboard side being placed first, then the corresponding pair on the port side and so on alternately. Examples of these methods of attachment are shown in fig. 153, where *A* shows a throat seizing on the bight, *B* an eye-splice.

FIG. 153.

Throat Seizing and Eye-splice.

On large scale models it is good practice to follow as far as is practicable the actual details of knots and splices and the arrangement that would be adopted on the real ship, but as a rule it is permissible to use very simple knots and to be content to reproduce the rope, and not bother too much about the kind of knot, as obviously it is a fiddly job to splice a No. 40 cotton; especially as a good appearance results from the use of adhesive in place of splicing, not a seamanlike method, but very practical for the average ship modeller.

FIG. 154.

The Rigging of the *Loch Torrens*.

In the case of *Loch Torrens*, fig. 154, a system of simplified rigging has been adopted, which cuts out a lot of the difficulties but retains sufficient accuracy and a marked degree of realism. The whole of the standing rigging for *Loch Torrens* is shown on plate No. 4, but it should be noted that corresponding ropes and shrouds on masts and other places that are similarly rigged have not been duplicated on the drawings, with the object of keeping the drawing as clear and explicit as possible, but obviously the ropes must be repeated for each corresponding part.

In addition to the standing rigging some of the running rigging is also shown on plate No. 4 for convenience and clarity. The names of the chief rigging shown on plate No. 4 are as follows:—

A Foreroyal stay
B Fore topgallant stay
C Flying jib stay
D Jib stay
E Fore topmast stay
F Forestay
G Mainstay
H Main topmast stay
J Main topgallant stay
K Main royal stay
L Mizen royal stay
M Mizen topgallant stay
N Mizen topmast stay
O Mizen stay
P Jigger mast stay
Q Jigger topmast stay
R Jigger topgallant stay
S Jigger royal stay
T Fore shrouds
U Fore topmast shrouds
V Fore royal shrouds
W Upper topsail lift
X Upper topsail downhaul
Y Martingale
Z Bobstay
A A Dolphin striker
B B Fore royal backstay
C C Fore topgallant backstay
D D Fore topmast backstay
E E Main lift
F F Royal lift
G G Lower topsail lift
H H Upper topsail tye
J J Royal yard rope
K K Footrope
L L Peak halliards
M M Vangs
N N Sheets
O O Topgallant yard rope
P P Upper topsail halliards
Q Q Throat halliards
R R Sheer pole.

At this stage, and before actually starting the rigging, it will be convenient to consider the various blocks and tackles that will be required and the method of arranging them. For all practical purposes, the blocks used are the ordinary commercially made wooden ones of the smallest size and fig. 155 shows several useful patterns. The plain single blocks are mostly required, say about 14 dozen in all, some plain double blocks about 3 dozen, a few of both kind but stropped that is fitted with a wire binding and a small hook are also advisable, say, 2 dozen single stropped and 2 dozen double stropped blocks. Dead-eyes and rigging screws have already been mentioned, and a few special patterns will be mentioned later on in their proper place, and will in any case have to be specially made. It is preferable to purchase the blocks ready for use as they are tedious to make in

Fig. 155.
Types of Model Ships' Blocks.

quantities and are inexpensive to buy; useful alternatives for small blocks are very small glass beads. If they must be made, it is best to fashion them from strips of boxwood, of correct section, as shown in fig. 156 and scored on each side with the corner of a chisel or point of an awl for the rope to reeve through the holes, known as "swallows." The holes

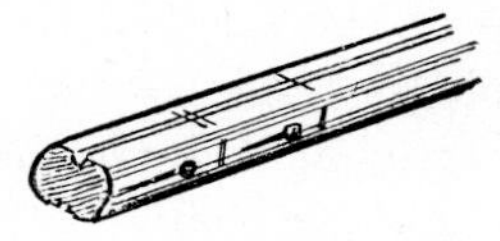

Fig. 156.
Making Small Blocks.

are then pierced by drilling, and the chases or grooves leading to them scratched in with an awl. The strip is then cut up, and the ends of the blocks completed by filing or shaping with a knife. They can also be made in a similar way from ebonite, erinoid or from knitting needles. Dead-eyes can be done in much the same way, using turned boxwood rods, grooved on the outside, cut to length and then drilled.

The tackles employed on *Loch Torrens* are shown in fig. 157 and comprise a runner *A*, single whip *B*, simple purchase *C*, lift purchase *D*, and a block with long wire strop *E*, used for direct attachment to a spar.

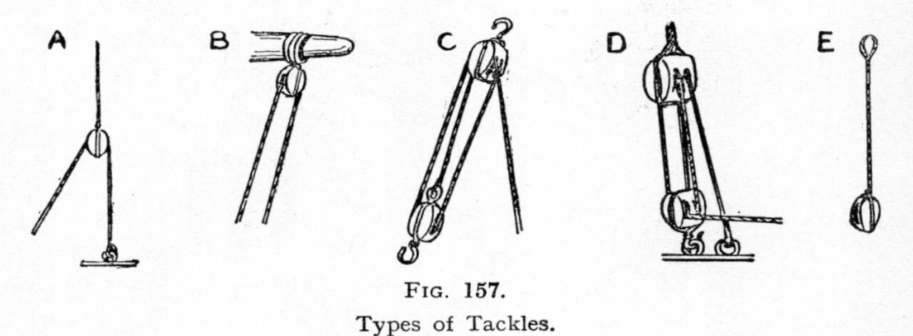

FIG. 157.
Types of Tackles.

The runner *A* has a single block with a rope attached to it, the second rope reeves through the block, one end is standing, that is fixed to an eye-bolt or elsewhere, the other end is free and is hauled in as required. The single whip *B* is similar but the block is usually stropped to a spar. The simple purchase *C* has a single block with strop or hook, and a double block with a rope attached. The lanyard or rope reeved through the blocks is free at one end, and the other attached to the strop of the single block. The lift purchase tackle *D* has two double (or triple) blocks, the lower is standing, the upper stropped or shackled to the rope, the lanyard, reeves through both blocks, one end is standing to an eye-bolt, the other is free.

These or similar tackles are quickly made by first carrying the rope to the block, preparing the lower block and reeving the lanyard through them. The word lanyard is here used in a descriptive sense while dealing generally with tackles for simple models and to designate the second rope; actually the ropes will be called by the name of the part they support or move as the case may be.

Dealing now with the specific work on the standing rigging for *Loch Torrens* it will be convenient to make the shrouds, and this is done quite simply and effectively in the following way.

Prepare a piece of card by drawing upon it the outline of the six shrouds spacing them according to the drawing plate No. 4, doing this as follows:—Near the upper part of the card piece a hole corresponding to the position where the shrouds will surround the mast. At the correct distance from this hole, draw the sheer pole (*R R* on plate No. 4), and along this line mark the spacing of the shrouds. Draw lines

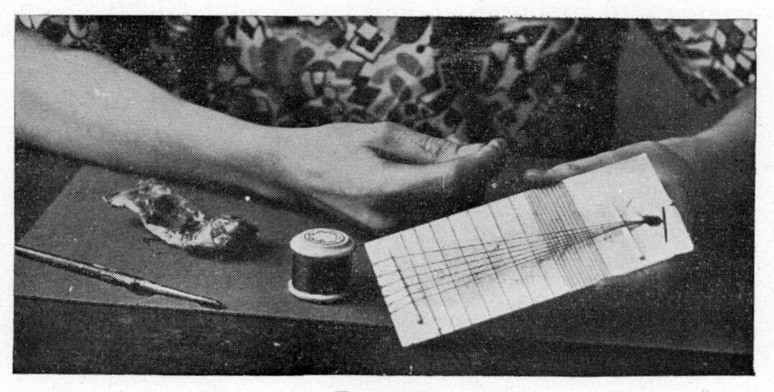

FIG. 158.
Making Shrouds and Ratlines.

through each of these marks to the upper hole and extend the lines downwards to the lower edge of the card, and cut notches in it at those points. Now set off the correct spacing of the *ratlines* or horizontal ropes which are attached to the shrouds, drawing a thick line at every fifth ratline.

Next take a length of thick black thread and wind it through the hole down to the first notch, up at the back of the card, through the hole and down to the second notch and so on, until all six are placed.

Now insert a match stick under each end of the shrouds as shown in fig. 158 and proceed to wind a thin cotton round and round the card, spacing it according to the marks shown on the card and continue until all the ratlines are complete. Prepare an adhesive solution of seccotine dissolved in water and brush it on to the whole of the shrouds and ratlines and leave it for a while to dry. Then cut the shrouds about the middle of their length on the *back* of the card, and with a sharp pair of scissors cut all the ratlines along the outside of each of the outer shrouds. This releases the whole, and it only then remains to clip out the four ratlines between each fifth ratline, as the ratlines stretch across the foremost five shrouds and only each fifth ratline (called a catch ratline) extends to the aftermost shroud. The result is a completed set of shrouds and ratlines; it looks neat and effective, and is quite strong if handled with reasonable care.

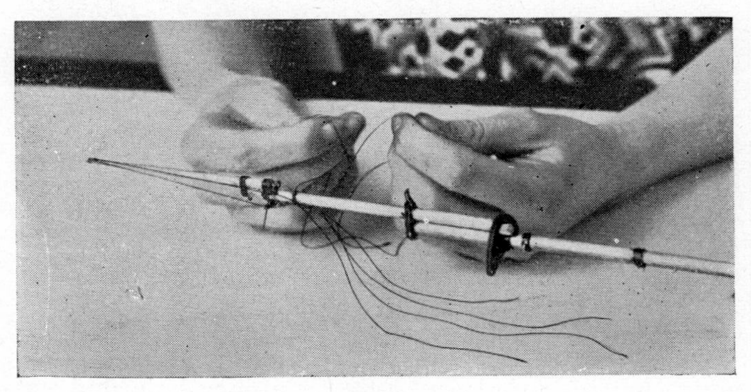

FIG. 159.
Fixing Topgallant and Royal Shrouds.

Two sets made in this way are needed for each lower mast, that is eight in all, and the time taken to make them is far less than setting up one set of shrouds on the model and then sewing on each ratline separately. Prepare the topmast shrouds in a similar way.

We can now commence rigging the masts, by fitting the topgallant and royal shrouds as shown in fig. 159 to the first three masts. Two lengths of cotton are tied around the top of the royal mast, the two pairs of ends brought down to the ends of the crosstrees, one pair on each side, and thence taken a little below the crosstree and lashed to the topmast with several turns of cotton. The shrouds are then drawn tight and all made fast and tidy with a touch of black varnish, and after it has dried the surplus ends are clipped off.

The topmast shrouds are then placed in position as shown in fig. 160 by passing the upper bundle of shrouds between the two masts, over the crosstrees, and then passing the three lower ends through the holes in the lower top, and fastening them to an eye-bolt in the mast band beneath the top.

FIG. 160.
Placing Topmast Shrouds.

The other set is then placed similarly on the opposite side, and the two upper bundles drawn tight and secured with a touch of seccotine; when dry the surplus clipped off close to the mast. The lower shrouds are then placed in position, passing them up through the lower part of the topmast shrouds beneath the top (called the futtock shrouds), through the lubber's hole in the top and between the masts as in fig. 161 through a hole drilled between them for that purpose an operation easily performed, with the aid of an

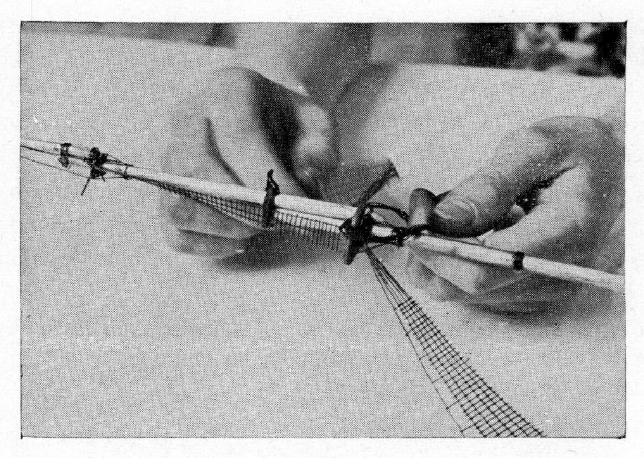

Fig. 161.

Fixing Lower Shrouds through the Top.

assistant, using the hand drill in the vice as shown in fig. 162 while the other manipulates the masts. Treat all three masts alike, and then rig the jigger mast in a similar manner, but pass the upper shrouds—which are single like the royal shrouds—through the holes in the ends of the jigger crosstrees. The lower shrouds are similar to the other but have five only,

Fig. 162.

Drilling a Hole between the Masts.

the odd forward shroud being omitted when making them, or can be cut off afterwards.

Now fit up the bowsprit with a pin as a dolphin striker, and fit the martingale, which is made of floral wire as shown in fig. 163, fastening the outer end with an eye on the wire, drawing the wire tight, twisting it around the dolphin striker at the lower end, fastening the other end of the wire to an

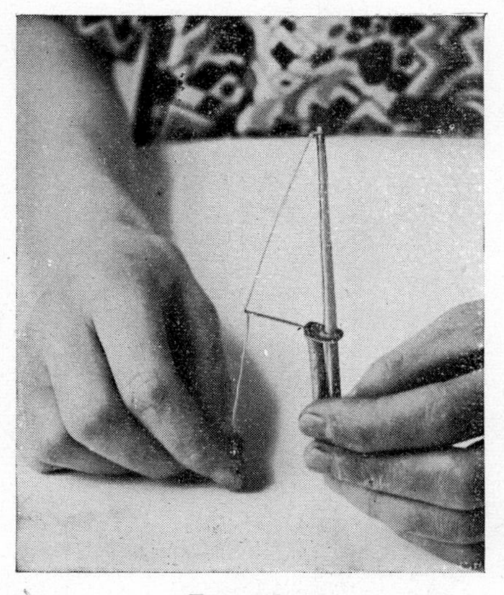

Fig. 163.
Fitting the Martingale.

eye in the stem of the hull as is clearly seen in fig. 164, which also shows the bobstay and jib guys. After the headstays have been permanently fixed the martingale is removed from the jibboom end and refixed at its proper place as shown on plate No. 4. The bowsprit steps into a hole drilled in the fore end of the hull immediately above the stem.

Now step the foremast, and fit the fore royal stay as shown in fig. 164, commencing with an eye around the mast at the top passing it through a pin hole in the end of the jibboom, passing the wire once around the jibboom, then forming a small loop in the wire, on the top of the jibboom—which will be wanted later on—and taking the wire temporarily to an eye on the bows as shown and there fastening it off

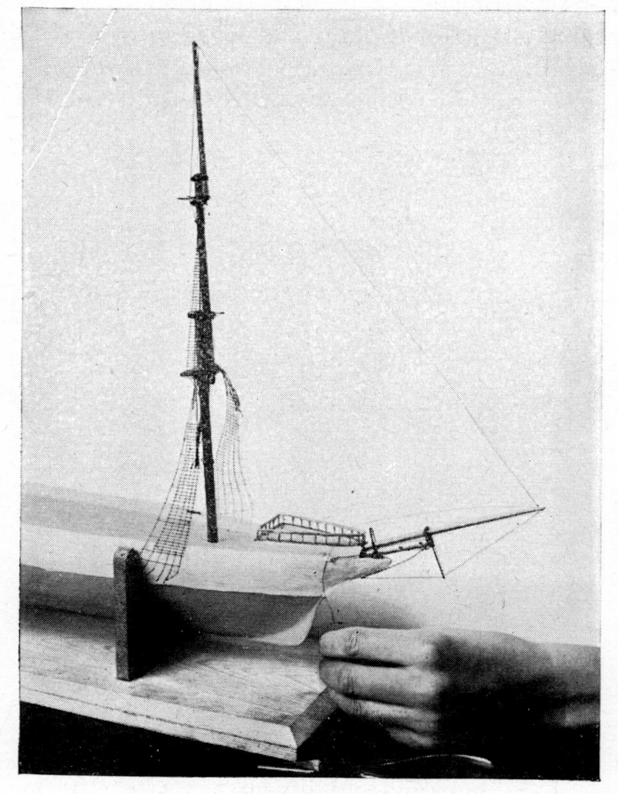

FIG. 164.
Fitting the Fore Royal Stay.

by twisting the free end around the other part but leaving an inch or so to spare.

The forestay is now prepared and placed, and is looped around the masthead above the shrouds, the lower end just above the handrails is formed into an eye. A piece of No. 28 gauge D.C.C. copper wire, painted black, is excellent for this purpose. A U-shaped piece of the same wire is attached to eyes driven into the sides of the stem as is shown in fig. 165.

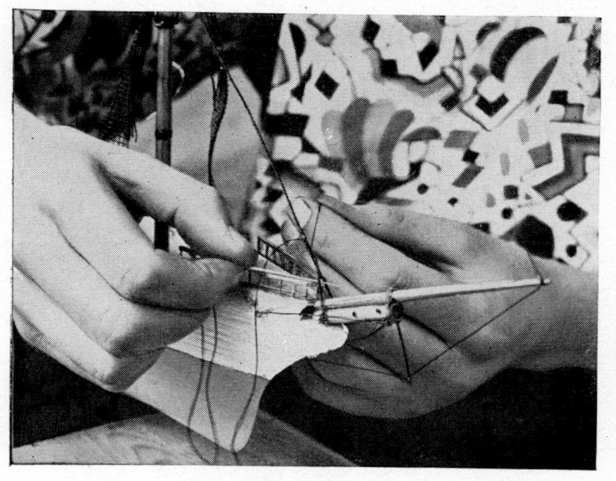

FIG. 165.
Fitting the Forestay.

Now fit the pair of royal backstays, making it from a length of floral wire, looped around the mast with a "throat seizing on the bight," represented by twisting the two parts of the wire to form an eye around the top of the royal mast. Draw the wires taut and twist them once around the spreaders one to each—and at the extreme end—then pass the free end through an eye in the deck and draw it taut and fasten off as before. Steady the mast as shown in fig. 166 while doing this work, and remember that it is these three wires that do most of the work of supporting the masts on the model. Adjust them as requisite to get all three taut, and to hold the mast at the proper rake.

Next tighten up the forestay with a lanyard of cotton passed several times through the eye, and the bight of the lower stay as shown in fig. 165, and then fasten off by turning the ends several times around the lanyard. Now fix the lower ends of the shrouds either with dummy rigging screws and eye-plates, or preferably as shown in fig. 167 by piercing holes in the angle between the deck and bulwarks at the correct spacings and pegging the ends of the shrouds with pointed match sticks. This allows of adjustment as requisite, after which the upper bundle of shrouds are drawn tight as shown

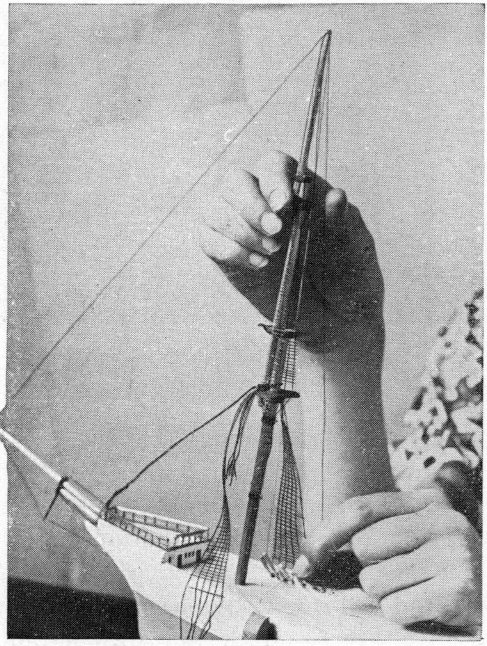

FIG. 166.
Fixing Fore Royal Back Stay.

and the opposite set similarly fitted; both are then drawn tight and secured with a touch of seccotine and a little wedge, and the surplus cut off. Leave the pegs as they are, and similarly step and rig the remaining masts, then remove the masts bodily with their shrouds and stays, while other work, including finishing the painting of the hull, is put in hand.

In practice, this plan will be found very convenient as it

then becomes possible to hoist the yards and complete a certain amount of the remaining rigging while the masts are free and more readily handled than is the case when they are stepped.

Later on when the masts are finally stepped and rigged, all the work already done will be a great help, as it is then only

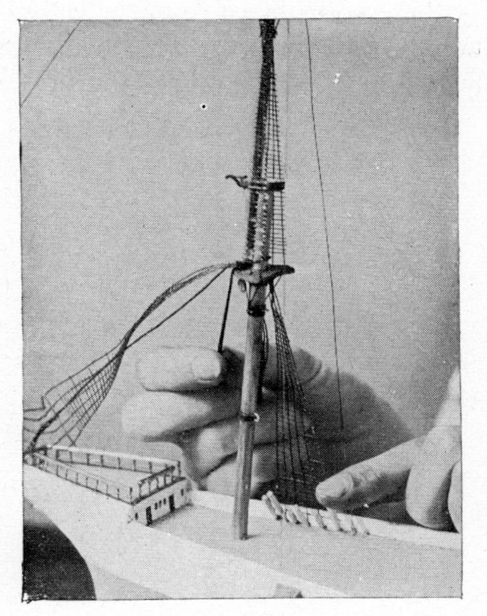

FIG. 167.

Fixing Shrouds to the Deck.

necessary to peg the lower ends of the shrouds, using a trace of adhesive on the points of the pegs, and afterwards to cut them off neatly. They are then almost invisible as only the fine point of the peg actually goes into the hull and sufficiently to hold the shrouds.

The remaining lower stays are then fitted similarly to the forestay but set up to eye-plates on deck, the upper stays can be of wire and set up directly from point to point as shown on the drawings, the remaining backstays setting up as already described for the fore royal backstays.

A point to note when finally fixing the headstays is that each one is twisted around the dolphin striker and thence taken to the eyes in the bows, and the martingale fixed in its proper place, it has to be temporarily fixed at the extreme end of the jibboom to take the pull of the fore royal stays. A pair of jib guys have to be fitted from the end of the jibboom to eyes in the hull near the bow, but these and other details can clearly be seen in fig. 154 showing the *Loch Torrens* fully rigged.

CHAPTER XII.

THE SAILS.

THIS IMPORTANT PART FULLY DEALT WITH—ALTERNATIVE METHODS AND MATERIALS DESCRIBED AND EACH SAIL ILLUSTRATED.

THE names usually employed to designate the various parts of a sail are as follows:—

Head—the top of a sail; *Leech*—the side of a sail; *Luff*—the weather leech or side first touched by the wind; *Foot*—the bottom of a sail; *Clews*—the two lower corners of a square sail and the after lower corner of fore and aft sails. *Tack*—the foremost lower corner of a fore and aft sail; *Tack* is also the name given to a rope attached to the foremost lowest corner of a course. *Peak*—the upper and aftermost corner of a spanker or trysail; *Throat*—the upper and foremost corner of the spanker or trysail; *Roach*—the curve in the foot of a sail; *Slab*—any slack part of a sail that hangs down.

There are in addition a number of ropes, strengthening bands of canvas and other details on real sails that are seldom shown on a model, including *Head Earings*, ropes spliced into the head cringles to secure a sail to the yardarm. *Reef-bands*—sewn across a sail to take the reef points or lines. The more important ropes used in handling a sail are named as follows:—

Sheets—to spread the lower corners of a square sail, other than a course, and the after lower corners of fore and aft sails, and a course; *Buntlines*—secured to the foot of a sail for taking it in or reefing; *Clewlines*—attached to the clews

FIG. 168.

Bow View of *Cutty Sark* Model Completed.

of square sails, except a course, when the corresponding rope is called a clewgarnet; *Downhaul*—attached to a sail to enable it to be hauled downwards.

The names of the sails are given in Chapter II., page 18, but there were additional sails used on some early clippers, notably studding sails, which were set outside the square sails and spread at the top upon yards and at the bottom by booms, both spars being supported in irons on the yardarms and by suitable rigging.

Working models intended actually to sail on a pond or other waters must necessarily have sails which can easily be trimmed and adjusted according to the needs of the moment. These conditions are not found in the average model clipper ship, which for reasons given elsewhere can never be a success as a working scale model.

Consequently in a consideration of the sails and sailmaking for models of the classes dealt with in this book the first requisite must be character and a pleasing appearance.

The sails for most scenic models are made of paper, but can be of any thin fine material such as voile, silk, handkerchief cambric and the like, and either left plain or decorated with lines to simulate the separate strips of which a real sail is composed. On a scenic model it is generally desired to make the sails appear as if bellying out and full of wind, which desirable effect can be obtained in several ways. The edges of the sails can be furnished with thin stiff wire curved to appropriate shapes, or the clewlines and buntlines can be of fine wire and adjusted to cause a paper sail to bulge out in the desired manner. In the case of sails made of fabric, similar results are obtainable by various means, including the impregnation of the material with superfine plaster of Paris, applied before the sail is hoisted. It is then hoisted carefully and sprayed with water from a scent spray or atomizer, and then a blast of air from a bellows or other convenient source is directed upon it from a suitable position.

Fig. 169.

Stern View of *Cutty Sark* Model Completed.

FIG. 170.—Broadside View of *Cutty Sark* Model Completed.

Under the force of the air the sail is caused to belly out in a natural manner and as the plaster of Paris dries the sail hardens and becomes permanently set. Another plan is to immerse the sail in very diluted solution of seccotine, and the sail hoisted and dried under air pressure as before. A variation of this plan is to moisten the sails one by one with the seccotine solution, or with a very dilute solution of clear white shellac, and again dry the sails in a current of air, or model them with a spoon as they are drying.

Opinions are divided as to the best treatment for the sails on a scale model, some prefer them plain, as shown on the *Stonehouse* model, fig. 3, in Chapter I., page 5; others prefer a slightly conventional treatment to suggest a curvature as in the case of the splendid model of *Cutty Sark* shown in figs. 168, 169, 170, where a certain feeling of life is imparted by simple curvature of the sails.

Incidentally these three illustrations will be found most helpful to all ship modellers on account of their clarity and completeness.

Whenever any sail is to be curved or bulged it is necessary to allow an extra amount on the depth to compensate for the curvature.

Paper is the easiest material for the novice to handle and is used on the *Loch Torrens*, as shown in fig. 171, and it does not stretch or pull, like silk or loosely woven fabrics; moreover, there are no such difficulties as the making of tiny hems while sewing is almost entirely eliminated. Many kinds of paper can be pressed into service for sails, but a common kind that is not quite dead-white looks very well, especially if it has a slight canvasy texture. Small models look well when the sails are made of fine crepe paper, Japanese rice paper or of soluble toilet paper of a pale straw colour, while for larger models a parchment or a common cartridge paper looks very effective especially when the seam lines are lightly indicated by pencil lines, and a slightly deeper tinge imparted to the edges by means of water colour paint to

FIG. 171.—Starboard Bow View of *Loch Torrens* Completed.

represent the tabling and the ropes at the edges—called the bolt-ropes.

Should it be decided to use a woven material it is essential to ensure that the edges will not fray out. This can be overcome in several ways, and especially on comparatively large models by means of neat hemming representing the tabling on a real sail, or by carefully sewing on a binding of baby ribbon or Prussian binding as shown in fig. 172, which is, however, not so easy as it sounds and looks.

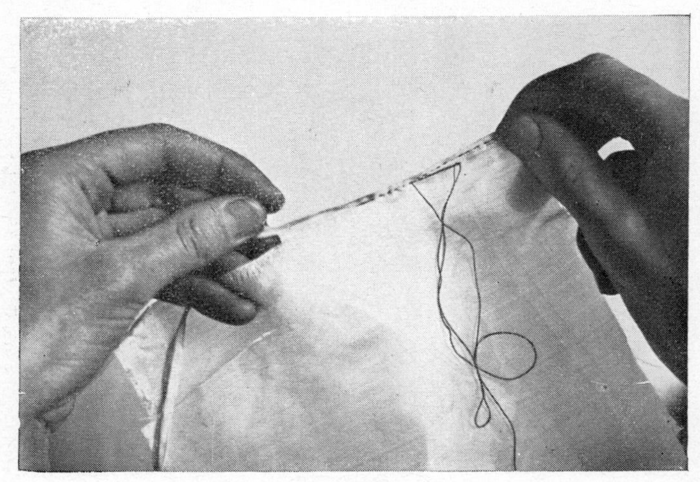

FIG. 172.
Sewing Binding to the Sail.

A clever seamstress is best qualified to do this work, and will not need any technical instruction, but others may find it helpful to clamp the sail between two thick pieces of card held together by strong paper clips as in fig. 173 to prevent the sail crinkling or pulling while the sewing is in progress. The need for either method is obviated by using such materials as taffetas, or by brushing the raw edges with a trace of gum water or clear white shellac dissolved in methylated spirits.

Whatever material is used, the grain or "way of the material" should always run from top to bottom of the sail in the case of square sails, be parallel with the leech or after side of triangular sails, and similarly disposed on a spanker, driver or rectangular trysail.

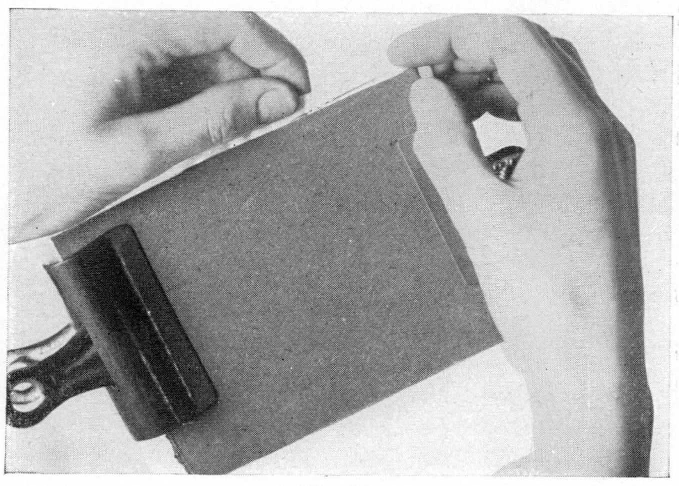

FIG. 173.
Use of Card and Clip while Hemming Sail.

As the *cloths* or strips of canvas of which a real sail is made measure about 18 to 24 inches wide any seams represented should be either machine stitched or drawn on the model sail at approximately the proper scale width.

Provided a model be made exactly to the designs, it is possible to cut the sails according to the sail plan, which for *Loch Torrens* is given on plate No. 3.

As a rule, however, some slight discrepancies creep in, and it is then desirable to hoist and rig all the yards and spars into their places and to make paper patterns to fit exactly, allowing for any desired curvature, as already mentioned. This should be done with caution, after checking by the drawings, or the spanker gaff may for example sag down a little as is apparent in one or two of the illustrations of *Loch Torrens*. The sails are set on the yards by sewing them to

Fig. 174.
Cutting Silk Sails.

Fig. 175.
Sewing Sail to Jackstay.

the jackstay, and spread at the clews by the sheets, consequently when cutting a sail pattern allow for it to reach the jackstay, but to leave a small gap between the clews and the yard beneath, to leave space for the block (if provided) and for the rope, or sheet; additional allowances must be made when cutting the sail if it is intended to be hemmed, otherwise it should be exactly to the pattern. To cut a fabric neatly is no easy matter, a good plan is to pin the material tightly

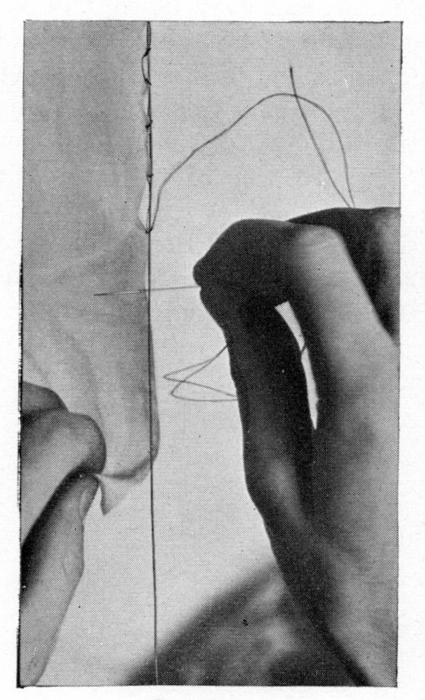

FIG. 176.
Sewing Headsail to Stay.

over a piece of cardboard, as shown in fig. 174, and to sever it with a razor blade. A simple wooden handle with a safety razor blade screwed to it as illustrated in fig. 174 is a very handy instrument especially as a new blade can be substituted when the first becomes dull.

Having cut the sails, and hemmed or otherwise completed them, they have to be provided with ropes, that is, cotton at the head wherewith to attach it to the upper yardarm, and the sheets may on most models be stitched directly to the clews leaving sufficient cotton or rigging cord to reach to the deck, or to the tackles as the case may be.

The sail can then be sewn to the jackstay as shown in fig. 175 with plain white or black cotton, passed through the sail, round the jackstay, down and through the sail, along a little way under the yard at the back of the sail, then through it, and up to the jackstay again and so on. In the case of headsails and staysails the weather leech is best attached to the stay by sewing, using a buttonhole stitch, or as shown in fig. 176, which illustrates the method used on *Loch Torrens*.

After the sail has been set the remaining ropes are reeved through the blocks, and the rigging completed as dealt with in Chapter XIII. on the Running Rigging.

CHAPTER XIII.

THE RUNNING RIGGING.

DEALT WITH IN A SIMILAR MANNER AND ILLUSTRATED WITH A FOLDING PLATE AND NUMEROUS LINE DRAWINGS AND PHOTOGRAPHS.

RUNNING rigging is the general term given to all the ropes used in handling the sails and spars, and roughly speaking can be thought of as movable ropes in contrast to the standing rigging, which is virtually a permanent fixture.

As already explained, the various ropes are all named according to the spar or sail they control, with the addition of a designating name. Thus a *halliard* is a rope, or chain, used to hoist a sail or spar on its appropriate mast or stay, and leads from it to the masthead. *Sheets* spread the foot of a sail, and in a square sail lead down from the clews to the yardarms; in a course they lead from the after clew to the ship's side; on staysails and headsails there are two sheets from the after clew, leading to each side of the ship. *Braces* are used to move a yard horizontally. *Lifts* support the yardarms to the masthead. *Vangs* are used to steady a gaff when the sail is brailed up, that is, taken in by the *brails* which lead from the after leech of the sail to the gaff or trysail mast. *Downhauls* are used for hauling down a sail or yard. As a general rule for running rigging all single ropes are secured to the yard or sail to be moved, and reeved, that is pass through the hole in a sheave or block secured at the place towards which it is to be moved, and from thence to the deck. *Yardrope* is the name of a single halliard used when raising an upper yard.

When sufficient power could not conveniently be applied by a single rope, it was customary to increase the power by incorporating some form of purchase tackle, as illustrated in fig. 157 in Chapter XI. This should be borne in mind while rigging, as the addition of such tackles appears to complicate the work and may otherwise lead to confusion. As a general guide it can be assumed that to double a single rope implies the placing of a single block at the point where the standing end, or fixed end, was attached. The rope is then reeved—that is, passed through the original block as before—then reeved through the new block and the standing end made fast near to the original block. For example, a simple single lift would have its standing end on the yardarm, and reeve through a block at the masthead, but when doubled the standing end would be on the masthead, and the rope be taken thence to the yardarm block, and back to the block on the masthead and then to the deck as before. A brace for an upper yard could be similarly dealt with but those on lower yards often have more complicated tackles. For example, a mainbrace could first be thought of as a single rope from yardarm to deck and could then be doubled as described above, but a further development is to remove the block from the yardarm, and secure it with an eye-splice to a short single rope, called a pendant, from the yardarm. Another rope is now reeved through this block, and one end made fast to the ship's side, the other end is provided with a block which forms the upper block of a tackle, the lower block of which is attached to the deck or ship's side. Consequently it is possible and permissible on a small model to make several minor modifications and simplifications without departing from the essential correctness of the rigging. This has been done to some extent—especially in relatively obscure or unimportant details—on the *Loch Torrens*, but the details of the running rigging as given on plate No. 3 and in figs. 177

and 179 should form an admirable basis for the novice. Those with the requisite knowledge and skill can add to or amend the details according to taste, inclination, or the purpose of their model.

It will be found convenient in practice to do as much of the running rigging as possible before stepping the masts, especially if the standing rigging be dealt with as described in Chapter XI. All blocks and pendants on the yards can be

FIG. 177.
Bow View of *Loch Torrens*

fitted, as well as the yard ironwork, and the yards themselves sent aloft, that is, be mounted in place on their masts, and lifts, yard ropes, halliards and sheets reeved and run as necessary, before the masts are finally stepped. The recommended procedure is to clothe each yard with all requisite blocks and fittings as shown on the drawings and plates Nos. 3, 4 and 5, then to hoist the yards and to add the lifts, etc., and afterwards to step the masts and complete the standing rigging. Then revert to the running rigging and finish it entirely.

FIG. 178.—Side View of *Sudbourne*.

The details and positions of the various blocks and ropes are given on the plates above, but those shown there all have to be repeated on port and starboard, and on all corresponding parts in a similar manner to the standing rigging. The drawings show every rope as far as is practicable while keeping the drawings as clear as possible, and if they are studied in conjunction with the side view of *Sudbourne*, fig. 178, period 1881, and the three quarter view of the *Loch Torrens*, fig. 179, and *Cutty Sark*, fig. 180, a tolerable notion of the rigging details should be obtained.

FIG. 179.
Stern View of *Loch Torrens*.

It would be impossible within the permissible limits of space to separately describe each of the ropes on *Loch Torrens*, nor will it be necessary if the foregoing general remarks, the information on the drawings and the following notes and photographic illustrations be carefully studied and followed as so many ropes are similar and disposed in the same way in corresponding parts.

Commencing with the yards, these should, where necessary,

FIG. 180.—Broadside View of *Cutty Sark.*

have the pendants attached to the yardarms as shown in figs. 181 and 188, which illustrate the single knot or loop employed for the purpose, the small loop is left for the sub-

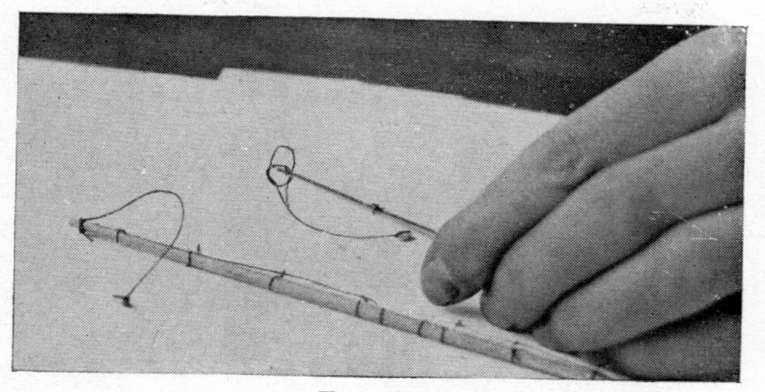

FIG. 181.
Fitting Pendant to Yard.

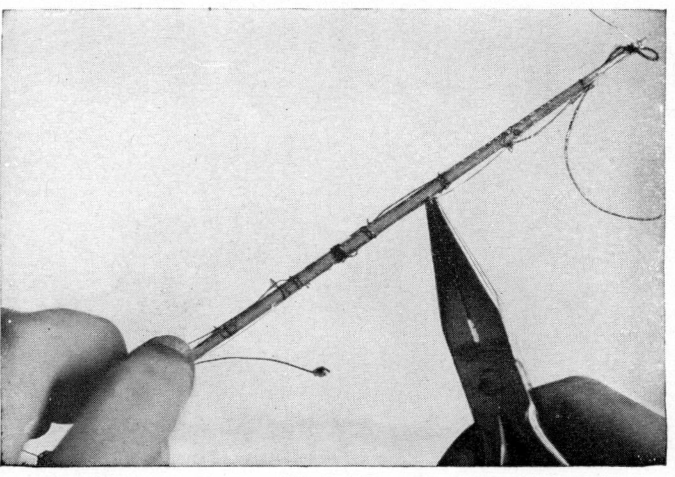

FIG. 182.
Fitting Jackstay.

sequent attachment of the lifts. The next step is to fit the quarter blocks and other blocks on the yard, and this is conveniently accomplished by stropping the blocks with cotton, that is, to tie the block into the bight of a loop of cotton leaving the two ends free, and then binding them twice around the yard, fastening with a knot and cutting off the surplus ends. Use the smallest possible blocks, and for many of them it will be found in practice that a long oval

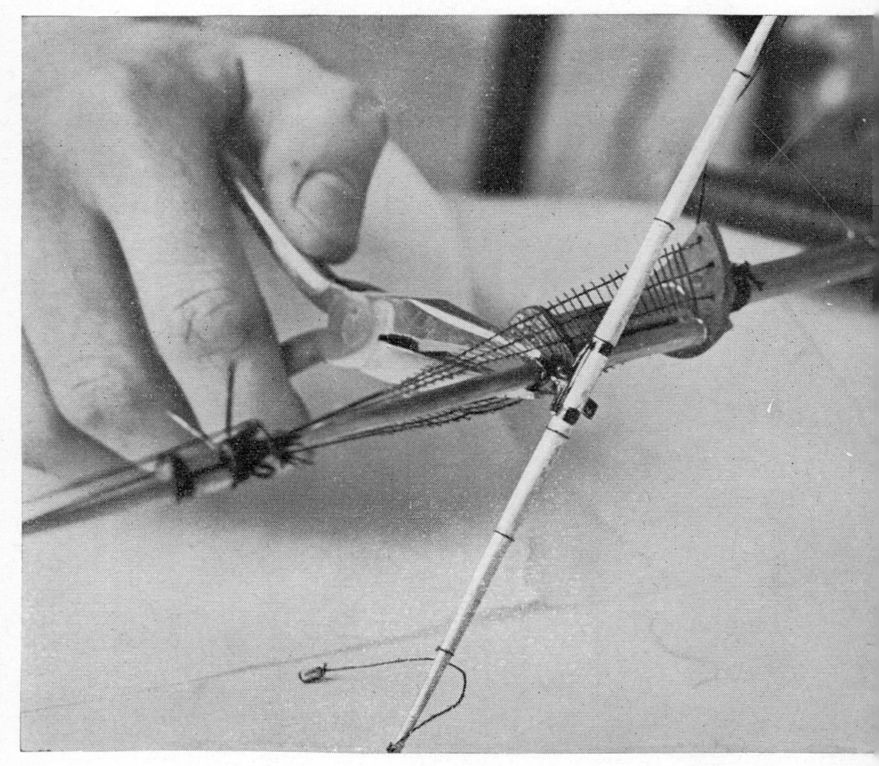

FIG. 183.
Fitting Upper Topsail Yard.

shaped but very small brown glass bead will both look well and work well, and is vastly easier to manipulate than a correspondingly small block.

Having fitted all the blocks, add the ironwork, parrels, or the like as requisite and then fit the jackstays, which for the *Loch Torrens* are made of floral wire, bound around the yardarm and lead along the top of the yard nearly to the centre and the end turned over and pressed into the yard; a few tiny staples of floral wire are then pressed into pin holes in the yard as shown in fig. 182 and thus hold the jackstay securely. It is best to do this work last as there is then less risk of bending or distorting the jackstay. Yard ironwork generally is fitted to the masts by opening the ring or eye, slipping the whole into place as shown in fig. 183, and closing the ring by carefully exerted pressure with the pliers. The next step is to connect the royal and topgallant yards to their yard ropes by twisting the end of the latter around the neck of the parrel. The yard ropes are preferably of floral wire and pass through holes drilled in the mast.

The upper topsail *tye* is fitted as follows. Attach a single block below the crosstrees, and another to the iron on the yard, fasten a cotton to the masthead, reeve it through the block on the yard, up through the other block and then through the hole in the mast, immediately below the crosstrees. About 2 inches below this point attach a block to the cotton, reeve a cotton through this block to form the halliards and attach one end to another block which is stropped to a short length of cotton fixed to the deck near the bulwarks, and reeve the other end of the halliards cotton through this lower block, and make it fast to a pin in the bulwarks. This tackle is clearly shown in fig. 184 and should be hauled on sufficiently to raise the yard to its proper place on the mast. The royal and topgallant lifts are dummy and simply consist of floral wire or cottons attached to the mast and to the yardarms. The upper topsail lifts reeve through a double block attached beneath the topmast crosstrees, and each terminates in a tackle like the upper topsail halliards.

The lower topsail lifts reeve through single blocks stropped to the topmast head, and terminate in a tackle as before. and the lower yard lifts are similarly arranged. The braces are next rigged up. those for the royals are single cottons from yardarm through a block on the after mast, the topgallant

N

braces have a simple tackle as shown on plate No. 3 made by attaching the standing end of the cotton to the after mast, reeving it forwards through the block on the pendant at the yardarm and thence back to the mast, through a block and down to the deck, belaying it to the bitts or pin rails.

FIG. 184.

Upper Topsail Halliards.

The upper topsail braces have a pendant block to which one end of a cotton is attached, and then reeved through a block stropped to the after mast, thence back through the pendant block and thence to the ship's side. The lower topsail braces are more complicated; one cotton reeves through the pendant block and has a standing end on the after mast, the other end is stropped to a block which forms the upper block of a purchase tackle, the lower block being stropped to the ship's side. The lower braces are a straightforward tackle, the pendant block has a cotton attached to it thence led down through the lower block which is stropped to the ship's side, up again through the upper block and thence through a block on the spider or on the ship's side and thence through the bulwarks and belayed to a cavil or stout post—represented by a peg at the side of the bulwarks. The spider is located on the ship's side near to the stern quarter as shown on plates Nos. 4 and 5 and is made from a stout pin partly driven into the ship's side. Three loops of floral wire are soldered to it at equal distances apart as shown on the left of fig. 185 and single blocks stropped into each. The ends

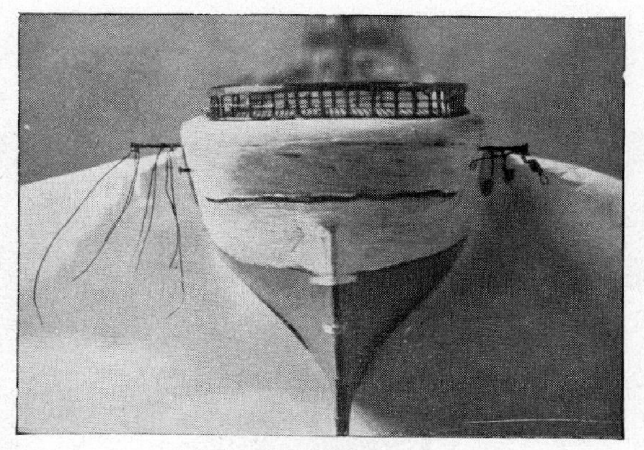

FIG. 185.
Details of Spider.

of the wires are formed into eyes to receive the standing ends of the tackles as shown on the right of fig. 185 and a single wire then soldered to the outer end of the pin, under the head, and taken aft and made fast by a short pin with head driven into the ship's side.

The sheets for the royal and topgallant sails are dummies on *Loch Torrens*, and lead from the sail, through a loop at the yardarm, to represent the usual sheave, and thence to the mast, behind their respective yards, but on a completely rigged model would be reeved through blocks or sheaves on the side of the yardarm and led down to the top or to the deck, as detailed on plate No. 3.

The upper topsail sheets reeve over pin heads in the yardarm to represent the sheeves, thence through the special double sheet block, and to the upper block of the whip or tackle. This block is made specially, and consists of a piece

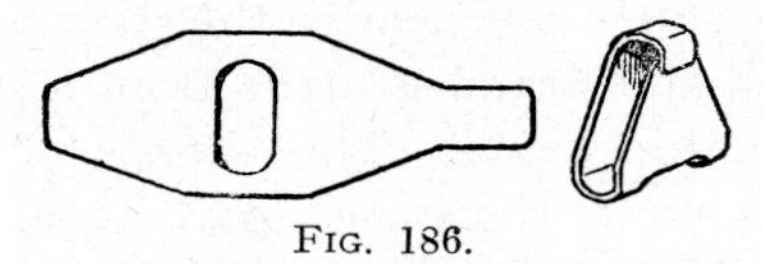

FIG. 186.
Upper Topsail Sheet Block.

of sheet zinc, cut to the shape shown in fig. 186, then bent up and the tab piece turned over and then attached to the hook beneath the upper topsail yard as shown in fig. 187; the

FIG. 187.
Upper Topsail Chain Sheets and Block.

detailed fitting is shown in fig. 107, Chapter IX. Usually the topsail sheets are made of chain and are so shown on ***Loch Torrens,*** but cottons or wire could be used instead.

The sheets on the lower sails comprise a block attached to the clew, and either shown as a single whip or as a tackle, the latter being detailed in plate No. 3 which clearly shows the arrangement of the ropes. The head and staysail sheets

FIG. 188.
Yards with Pendants Attached.

are directly attached to the clews of the sails, and are duplicated, one set going to port (left hand) and the other to the starboard (right hand) side of the ship, and can be single cottons or may have a whip attached.

The halliards for these sails lead from the upper corner of the sail to a block stropped to the mast, near to the stay and thence to the deck, leading some of them down through a block stropped to the shrouds as indicated on plate No. 5. By this time there will be a considerable number of ropes or cottons on the model and it is imperative to keep them all nice and taut but not strained in any way or the masts or yards may be bent. Another thing to be careful is to avoid accidental collisions of the hand with the rigging or damage

FIG. 189.
Showing way Halliards are Secured.

will result. Patience, the use of a crotchet hook, and the snout-nosed pliers will ensure success, and other useful hints are to draw each piece of cotton or rigging cord through a piece of beeswax to make it smooth and supple, also it often is a great help to use a needle or a length of floral wire, threading the cotton through it and then passing the needle from place to place as requisite. Downhauls on the head and staysails can be dummy, but are preferably combined with the halliards by attaching one part to the upper corner of the sail, then using the lower part to attach the sail to the stay, and reeving through the lower block and thence taking them, as with other sheets and halliards to the deck as shown in fig. 189 and belaying to the bitts or to pins in the bulwarks. The rigging of the jigger gaff and boom can be followed easily from plate No. 3 and 5 and from fig. 190 and no difficulties should be experienced here.

FIG. 190.
Rigging of Jigger Mast, Gaff and Boom.

The next step is to bend the sails to the yards by sewing them to their jackstays and similarly to sew the other sails to their stays, gaff or boom as the case may be. The buntlines, which should be of very thin cotton, are then placed, and lead from the foot of the sail on the fore side up through the block on the forward side of the yard, thence to a block on the mast near the masthead, and thence to the top or the deck, or they can terminate at the mast if preferred, and the leech lines are similarly disposed. The clew lines and clewgarnets are located on the after side of the sail and reeve through a small block on the clew of the sail, and through a block on the yard as shown in plate No. 3 and in several other illustrations.

The sheets can be directly attached to the clews of the sails when they are not made of chain, but in the latter event it is necessary to reeve the chain through a block attached to the sail and thence to an eye-bolt on the yardarm. Small blocks and fittings can be sewn directly to any sail when it is made of silk or other material, but when they are made of paper the cottons can be gummed neatly to the clews and then covered with little triangular tabs of thin paper, a system that makes them surprisingly strong. The spanker brails are dealt with in a similar manner to the bunt and clew lines on the square sails, but are on both sides of the sail. The remaining ropes are then dealt with on generally similar lines, and although it may sound a very difficult job while reading this chapter it will be found in reality to be far more straightforward particularly as each corresponding sail or yard is similarly rigged. All the work is progressive, and if a few mistakes are made they can always be rectified without any serious trouble.

The best plan is first to fit the yard ropes or halliards to raise the yards, then to add the lifts to keep them level, next deal with the braces to keep the yards from swinging around the masts, then rig the spanker, add the sheets for the square sails, then bend on the square sails and finish the bunt and clew lines and complete the work by bending and rigging the fore and aft sails. Finally go over the whole of the rigging, adjusting it as necessary and making any requisite alterations or additions.

CHAPTER XIV.

PAINTING AND FINISHING.

ILLUSTRATED WITH PHOTOGRAPHS AND LINE DRAWINGS, THIS CHAPTER SHOULD BE MOST USEFUL IN SECURING A WORKMANLIKE FINISH TO THE MODEL. EVERY IMPORTANT MATTER IS FULLY COVERED.

MUCH could be written on the subject of painting and finishing processes for model clipper ships, what should be done and what not done, but in practice the novice is confined to the use of ordinary commercial pigments and materials. There is nothing inherently different in the methods of painting a small model hull than there is in painting any other small object, provided each are equally well done.

In one respect the painting of a model boat hull differs from the ordinary kind of jobbing paintwork in that it is essential to build up a perfectly smooth surface devoid of brush marks. To attain this result the hull itself must be blameless, free from imperfections in carving, and must have a smooth uniform surface.

The novice should understand from the start that paint may cover a multitude of sins in the way of indifferent work, but it never conceals them; on the contrary the play of light on the curved surfaces reveals every little imperfection. The first step in finishing a model ship is therefore to begin well with the woodwork and to get the hull as perfect as possible.

Assuming this has been done and the woodwork to be clean and well sandpapered, commence operations by filling the grain with any good wood filler. A preparation made by Hobbies Ltd. was used on *Loch Torrens* and proved very efficacious; it is supplied in a paste form, and needs a little dilution with turpentine and is then well rubbed into the wood

Fig. 191.
Using Wood Filler.

as shown in fig. 191 with a pad of linen. Allow it to dry hard, which will take several hours, then go over the hull with sandpaper as in fig. 192 using an old worn piece, and work in all directions with a brisk but light action. One application is usually sufficient but a second coat can be given if the wood

Fig. 192.
Sandpapering the Hull.

appears to be porous or rough. On *Loch Torrens* the second joint from the top of the hull is exactly on the L.W.L., and it is as well to now draw a pencil line around it to serve as a guide when applying the darker colour paint below the waterline and the painting proper can be commenced with a coat of "priming," which can be either a good quality lead colour paint or a mixture of equal quantities of red and white lead, diluted with turpentine or gold size. This should be applied with a soft brush as in fig. 193 and well worked into the

FIG. 193.

Painting the Underwater Part.

wood. Leave this until it is thoroughly dry. This will take from twenty-four to thirty-six hours according to the time of the year.

If the colour below the waterline is to be darker than that above, it is well to paint only the below waterline part of the hull, brushing the paint very carefully along the pencil line, and when this coat is dry, apply a lighter shade to the part above, thus preserving the true line of the L.W.L.

The painting proper may continue by rubbing down the surface and giving other coats of grey or priming paint, followed when dry by careful sandpapering with fine old sandpaper until a very smooth surface is obtained. If the wood is particularly porous it may be advisable to give another coat of the priming or a plain lead colour paint. This again must be left until thoroughly dry, and then sandpapered until it is perfectly smooth.

The wood should now be ready to receive the desired

colour. At this stage either of two methods of finishing the work may be followed. The boat may be enamelled with any well-known enamel, and excellent results can be obtained from the use of good grade commercial preparations. Directions for use are always supplied by the makers, and should be followed exactly although a few points that should be borne in mind when using enamels are to apply a good but not too thick coating of colour, allow it to dry thoroughly hard, then very lightly sandpapering it or rub it down with pumice powder and water, then apply a second coat when the first is thoroughly hard, afterwards rub it down with pumice powder and water until a smooth polished surface is obtained. If a glossy finish is desired a third coat of enamel should be brushed softly over the surface, taking great care to use a clean brush, to apply the enamel evenly, and above all to work the brush in one direction and not backwards and forwards, as doing so causes the varnish in the enamel to lose much of its brilliance. The alternative process is one that gives the very best results, and is obtained by the use of paint known as "coach colour ground in oil." This can be obtained from most high-class oil and colour merchants, but must not be confused with the ordinary painter's colour ground in oil. Coach colour is much finer, and merely requires thinning down with turpentine to the required consistency, and then applied with a flat sable hair brush very evenly and lightly to the surface of the boat.

This colour usually dries in two or three hours, but it is not hard enough for polishing for at least twelve to twenty hours, according to the state of the weather. In wet, cold weather paint takes two or three times as long to dry hard as in warm weather. Five or six coats of this colour should be applied to work up a good body, and between each coat the work should be very lightly sandpapered and in the later stages should be rubbed down with pumice powder. Of course, while this rubbing down and polishing process is going on, the boat and brush must be kept well away from dust, and the work should be wiped down with a damp linen cloth and dried thoroughly with a clean dry cloth before applying the next coat of colour. The model should be hung up to dry, deck upwards, in a room as free from dust as possible. It is usually feasible to hang any model boat in this way, and is worth the trouble, as more dust settles on to a boat from above than rises up and settles upon the surface. When the boat has been finished thus far with the colour or colours, it must be varnished, and this requires both skill and practice. A good start is made by obtaining a small quantity of varnish of any reputable brand of which a little should be poured into a clean saucer, and using a small fairly stiff brush apply it with an easy but definite action.

The idea is to put on exactly the right amount of varnish at the start, and not to be compelled to brush away the surplus from one part to make up the deficit in another. Above all, the brush should be used only in one direction, usually from left to right, and the varnish must not be worked or brushed to and fro, as this causes it to cloud and so lose its pristine appearance. Two or three light coats give better results that one or two heavy coats. In six to eight hours the varnish may appear to be dry to the touch, but must be left *at least* 24 *hours* and probably longer before it is rubbed down with pumice powder, as if the varnish is not absolutely dry and thoroughly hard the heat generated by the polishing process will "lift" the varnish. Pumice powder can be purchased ready ground for use and is very much like dirty flour in appearance; to use it, a pad of soft linen should be made, dipped in water and then dabbed in the pumice powder. The pad is then rubbed lightly and with a circular motion on the hull, and after three or four turns this circling movement is continued and gradually carried forward over the whole surface of the model, frequently dipping the pad in water and using more pumice as required. Skill can be acquired by practice alone, but the result obtainable is well worth the trouble expended on it. A very beautiful effect is obtained by varnishing the boat with two or three coats of varnish and polishing the same between each coat, very lightly rubbing down the last coat with pumice powder applied by preparing the pad as already described, but covering it over with a single layer of linen. This is made thoroughly wet and used as a rubber. The pumice powder partially penetrates the outer linen covering, thus only very slightly dulling the surface of the varnish, giving it an appearance very much akin to glass. When it is desired to indicate the waterline, or to paint the hull in two or more colours, as in the case of *Loch Torrens*, some means of marking the divisions between the different colours is advisable. This can be accomplished in many ways, one is that of employing a scribing block to scratch-mark the waterline, but if a proper scribing block is not available a substitute may be made with a block of wood, through which has been driven a long metal point.

Any fairly large smooth piece of wood will answer, but it should be capable of free movement over the surface of a smooth table. To use it, the hull is supported with the L.W.L. parallel to the table, a hole drilled through the block at this level, and a metal peg, or even a hard lead pencil, pushed through. The block is then moved around the hull in such a way that the point will incise a line around it which will of course be at the L.W.L. level. Other levels can be indicated in the same way by raising or lowering either the hull or the pointer in the block. Several coats of colour will not obliterate this scratch-line, and with a steady hand and a small brush it is easily possible to draw a clean straight line defining the two different colours by working the paint carefully to this line.

Another way of indicating the lines of demarkation between different bands of colours on a hull is to immerse a thin cotton in diluted seccotine and carefully stick it to the hull. The paint is then easily applied and when dry the whole can be sandpapered as usual, the cottons remaining on the hull and ultimately become one with the colour, or may be removed and the succeeding coats of colour worked to the lines thus defined.

To satisfactorily paint a model boat in a high class manner requires considerable care and plenty of time to ensure the result being permanent, but it is well worth devoting sufficient thought and care, as it is generally admitted that good paintwork on a model sets off the fittings and adds very greatly to the resulting pleasure obtained from the boat.

In the case of deck erections, saloons and such like structures it is customary to indicate the windows with Prussian blue, or other colours to choice, and provided the woodwork has received a coat of priming and a light coat of flat white paint, it is quite possible to paint in the windows and so forth with ordinary water colour paints or with poster colours as used by artists, the utmost care is necessary however, in varnishing over such work, or the paint will be smeared. A light coat of thin spirit varnish is the best and is applied in the ordinary manner.

Exhibition or glass case models are generally finished and coloured with special spirit colouring media, and finally polished in a manner somewhat allied to French polishing, but it is beyond the scope of this book to detail these processes, as it requires a long apprenticeship to the trade to obtain complete success.

Simple cases and stands look well if stained a warm brown made by diluting Brunswick black with turpentine, and finishing when dry by a liberal polishing with any good furniture polish. Alternatively, the wood can be coloured with a water stain, or other suitable pigment and finally varnished or French polished; the latter is, however, a skilled job and usually beyond the skill of the novice.

Embellishments in the way of gold lines and so forth are best applied with liquid gold paints or with the transfers sold for lining bicycle frames and the like. Modelling in low relief such as is sometimes required on the counter and elsewhere on a clipper model can be worked in with "Gesso" or any of the various preparations on the market.

Scenic models with plaster waves and the like can be painted very effectively with ordinary poster colours, which are sold in tubes and bottles in the form of a paste and have to be diluted with water. They should be applied as soon as possible after the plaster has set but before it has dried out, otherwise it will be necessary to wash over the plaster with a large brush charged with clean water.

If oil colours are used the plaster should be allowed to stand for several days to harden, then be coated with shellac varnish and the oil colours applied after it has thoroughly dried.

Back-scenes, and other parts made of paper or Bristol board, are preferably painted with ordinary water colours but if great body or solidity in the colour is essential it is needful to work them with Chinese white, or to employ the poster colours.

Small metal parts look very well when electro-plated in dull silver or if oxydised and lacquered, work which can be done at small cost by any local electro-plating firm, an expense that is well justified by the resulting high grade appearance of the completed model.

than sandpapering the surface and possibly trueing the edges to make them square and correct to sizes.

See that all the specified pieces are cut square with the sides, then proceed to glue and nail two of the pieces B together at the edges to form an angle piece, and do the same with a second pair, thus making the two outer corner posts. Lay one of them, with the shorter part flat on the table, that is the piece which was nailed to the other should be on the table the longer part standing up in the air. This will be quite apparent when the work is actually in progress. Next lay two pieces E, one at the top and one at the bottom of the part on the table, and to their ends apply one piece B, glue the joint faces and secure them by 1-inch panel pins driven diagonally—called "cross nailing"—through the edges of the wood. See that everything is square and true, then glue and pin one of the pieces of plywood K, to the frame. Do the same with the other end, thus making the two panelled ends of the case. Lay them on the table with the panelled parts upright, and glue and nail the pieces D one at the top and one at the bottom to form the front part and the opening. Then glue and screw the whole to the top of the baseboard A. Add the pieces C to the front and back, by glueing and nailing to the top and fill in the gaps at the ends with the remaining two pieces E. Make the pediment from the pieces F and G by cutting both ends of F and one end of each of G to an angle of about 20°; mitre these angular ends, that is, cut their ends to an angle of 45° and also plane their under sides to a bevel, and so that they will fit flat on to the top of the case. Round off the upper edge of the pediment pieces and then glue and nail the whole in place as seen in figs. 194 and 195, the former showing the exterior and the latter the interior of the case made as above described.

The four square pieces H are then glued and nailed at the under side of the corners of the baseboard, and should project about $\frac{1}{4}$ inch on the front and side faces, but be flush at the back. The opening is glazed by placing the glass in position and securing it with strips of passe-partout binding—or with fillets or beads of thin wood. The back is made by screwing the piece of plywood J to the rear edges of the case, and the top enclosed by resting the ground glass on it, and securing it with passe-partout binding to exclude any dust.

The model simply slides into the case from the rear, and is secured by screwing on the back. If it is desired to illuminate the model, two or three ordinary electric bulbs can be fitted as indicated in fig. 195 by fastening ordinary batten holders

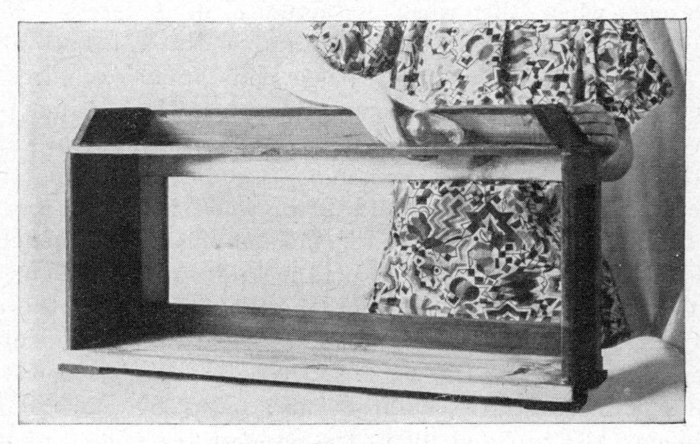

FIG. 195.
Interior of Scenic Model.

to the pediment and wiring them to a switch and plug connection in the usual way. The top is then preferably enclosed by a piece of plywood enamelled white on the under side, but the opening at the back of the pediment should be left open to provide sufficient ventilation.

This case looks very well if stained with Brunswick black diluted with turpentine, which yields a warm brown colour, preceded with a coat of wood filler and well sandpapered before staining and finally completed by dull polishing with any ordinary furniture cream.

A simple form of shade suitable for enclosing a collection of waterline models is shown in fig. 196 and is made with a lower frame of wood about 1¾ inch deep and ⅜ thick with a groove on the upper edge, wooden uprights about ¼ inch square are fixed to the inner corners and the pieces of glass then fitted

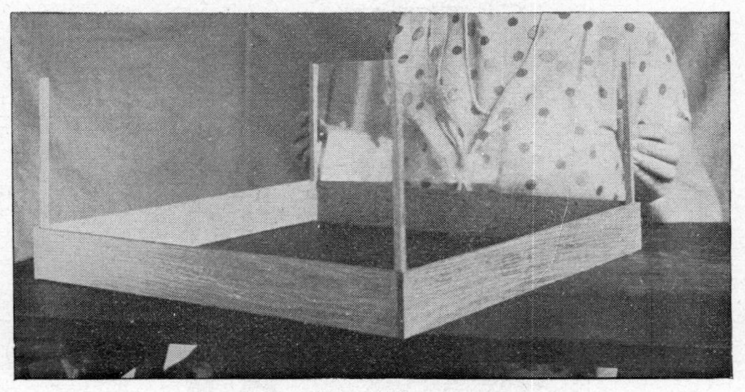

FIG. 196.
Making Case for Waterline Model.

into the grooves in the bottom frame, and secured at the corners with passe-partout binding, after which the top glass is rested on them and similarly fixed with a binding on the inside and on the outside.

A suitable case and stand for the *Loch Torrens* is shown completed in fig. 197 and is composed of the following pieces of ordinary commercial white deal obtainable at any timber yard at a total cost of about 7/6.

A—8 pieces 30 ins. long, 3 ins. wide, ½ in. thick.

B—12 pieces 36 ins. long, 3 ins. wide, ½ in. thick.

C—2 pieces 36 ins. long, 9 ins. wide, 1 in. thick.

These sizes are as before described the "nominal" dimensions, the above are for the stand.

The following are required for the glass case:—

D—4 pieces 20 ins. long, ½ in. square stripwood.

E—4 pieces 34 ins. long, ½ in. square stripwood.

F—4 pieces 14 ins. long, ½ in. square stripwood.

and twice the above quantity of stripwood ¼ in. wide, ⅛ in. thick and the same lengths.

The material sold by Hobbies Ltd. and known as stripwood is excellent for this purpose; the writer used satin walnut but other woods are available if preferred.

FIG. 197.
Case and Stand for *Loch Torrens*.

The stand is of modern design with a certain Eastern suggestion about it as befits a clipper ship model, and is readily made in the following way as all joints are merely butted, glued and nailed with panel pins, and is surprisingly rigid and strong when the whole is completed.

First assemble the legs, by making the 8 pieces A into four angles as shown in fig. 198 previously described, but round off the outer corner with a plane, and make it smooth with sandpaper. Next glue the two boards C together edge to edge, and cut two pieces of the remaining wood B, long enough to reach across the two boards, terminating ½ inch inside each edge. Fix these battens at ½ inch from each end, then hold one of the legs upright at the corner, pressing it against the batten, get an assistant to hold the opposite leg and measure the exact distance between their inner edges. Cut a piece of wood to fit closely between them, and try it in place as shown in fig. 199 and do the same for the other pair of legs, and mark all of them to ensure their replace-

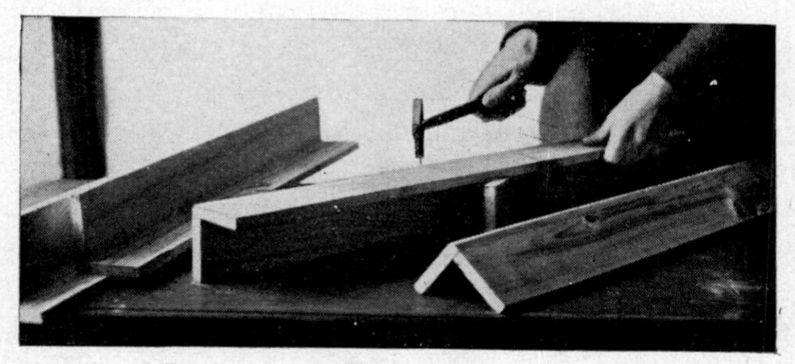

Fig. 198.
Assembling the Legs of the Stand.

Fig. 199.
Leg and Top of Stand.

ment in their proper places. Similarly measure off and cut two long pieces to reach between the front and back edges of the legs, and mark them as before. Lay the front pair of legs flat on the table, and the long piece between them at the top. Then cut two pieces each 12 ins. long, 9 ins. long and

6 ins. long, and assemble them into the corners as shown in fig. 200 and prepare a diagonal brace to reach from the leg to the top piece, using the same material, as the 36-inch lengths B on the list, will be found to cut up with very little waste. Glue and screw the brace to them and treat the other leg in the same way and similarly make up the back pair of legs to correspond. Plane or sandpaper the faces until they are smooth, and then assemble them by glueing and nailing to the two bearers and the top board. Then fix the cross pieces at the end, and also the additional corner pieces which are $7\frac{1}{2}$ ins. deep, and set with the grain parallel to the legs.

FIG. 200.
Assembling the Front Lower Portion of Stand.

Allow the whole to dry, then round off the corners of the top boards, sandpaper everything quite smooth, and fill the grain with wood filler. Give the whole two coats of Berlin black, and when dry apply the decorative panels which are cut from silver paper used in cigarette cases, and secure them by painting the back of the silverfoil with Berlin black, and pressing them firmly into contact.

The glass case is made by laying two pieces E flat on the table and two pieces F between them at the ends to form a frame. Glue and nail them together and take every care to keep them flat and square. Round off one corner of the other pieces E and F and glue and nail them together with the rounded corners outwards and upwards. Both of these frames must be exactly alike when laid on top of one another. Next round off one corner of the pieces D and glue and nail them between these frames at their corners. Allow the whole to dry hard, then round off the odd corners, give the whole a careful rub over with sandpaper and paint it with Berlin black. Have five pieces of good quality window glass cut to fit *exactly* but not tightly into the side and top openings and secure them with the narrow stripwood beads,

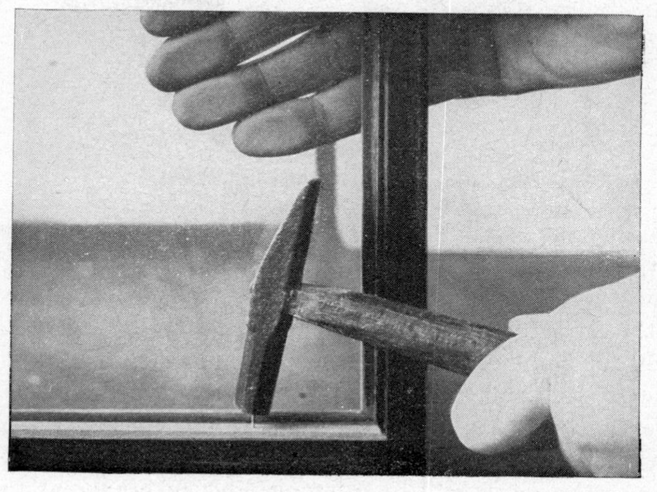

Fig. 201.
Fixing the Bead to the Case.

$\frac{1}{4}$ inch wide, $\frac{1}{8}$ inch thick, one set being glued flush with the inside and set vertically and secured here and there with pin points. The other bead which comes on the outside is laid flat and secured with pin points after the glass has been fixed as shown in fig. 201, but the beads should be blacked before fixing: they were left plain for the photograph to make them apparent.

The case is held in position on the stand by four corner pieces of wood, triangular in shape, which can best be fixed before the glass is fitted to the framework, as they should come neatly in the inner corners, and when blacked are quite inconspicuous.

Prepare two blocks or small supports made from odd lengths of the stripwood as in fig. 202 to represent the heavy baulks

FIG. 202.
Supporting Blocks for Finished Model.

of timber on which a ship rests when in dry dock, shaping their upper edges to fit the hull. Screw them to the hull with a fine screw through each and place the model in position on the stand. Prepare and fix a neatly lettered tablet giving the name of the ship, her approximate date of building, name of the maker and any other interesting information; place the glass case over the model, and if everything has been done with ordinary common sense and painstaking patience the result will be a lasting joy, an ornament to any room and a tribute to the skill and ability of the maker.

CHAPTER XV.

FINDING THE INFORMATION.

How to Find the Necessary Data for the Construction of Any Type of Clipper Ship—The Use of Photographs and Other Illustrations and so Forth—A Bibliography is Included—Index.

The necessary data and information for the construction of a model clipper ship depends entirely upon the class of model to be built.

A waterline or scenic model requires only a few leading dimensions and a good broadside view of the prototype together with an illustration of her under sail, as for instance racing before a strong wind which would form a splendid guide when making a scenic model.

A good scale model with complete detail would, however, necessitate a set of hull lines, sail and rigging plans and several views of the deck gear. The difficulty is to acquire this information, where and how to begin, especially when the ship-modeller is not a seafaring man or in close touch with nautical affairs.

Suppose for the sake of example that it is desired to model an early ship on which some member of the family had served in years gone by, but the name only is known. The first thing to do is to find out the date when she was in commission, say 1868 for example. Then it may be found for instance that she sailed to China, and it would be safe to infer she traded in tea, silk or some other Eastern produce. This prompts a search for books on sailing ships of about that period that traded to China. Consequently look up such works as *Lloyd's Register of Shipping*, Lubbock's *China Clippers*, and any others on the subject. Here may be found some mention of her, or her date and place of building; if so a letter to the makers, if still in business, is the next step, and so on gradually following up one clue after another until her leading dimensions are known and a picture of her is located. A photograph can often be found in the stocks of the regular marine photographers.

Now comes the preparation of some outline drawings, but immediately there arises the question as to how they are to be transferred to paper, and how the dimensions and proportions are to be ascertained. A fair start can be made by drawing an horizontal line on a suitable sheet of white paper, and on it marking off the actual length of the waterline of the model itself if it is not more than say 24 to 30 inches long, but for larger models it will suffice if the drawings are half full size.

For convenience, suppose the drawing is full size, and that the model is to be made to a scale of 1/10 inch equals one foot. Suppose it is known that the original ship is 210 feet long, the beam 36 feet and depth 21 feet. It may not be clear if the length means the overall length of the hull from taffrail to stem head, the length between perpendiculars, or the load waterline line length, but if an average is taken and the scale length of 205 feet be marked on the waterline the error cannot be very much, consequently a length of 20½ inches is set off along the horizontal line.

The depth probably refers to the depth from maindeck to keel, and observation of contemporary drawings will show that about two-thirds will be below the L.W.L. and one-third above, therefore set off a depth of 1·4 inches below the line and draw another to indicate the bottom of the keel. Then draw another horizontal line above the L.W.L. at a distance from it of ·7 inches. Now study the available illustrations

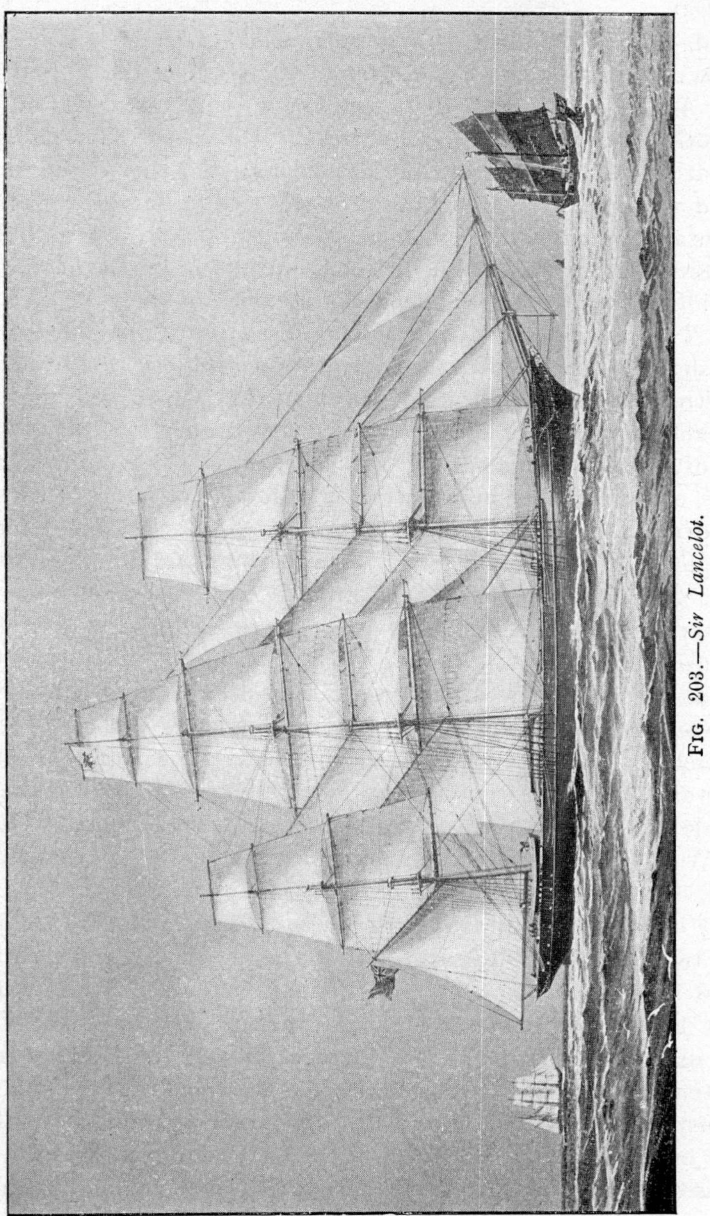

FIG. 203.—*Sir Lancelot.*

and, guided by them, draw the outline of the bows, stern, and a good easy curve to represent the sheer of the toprail.

At a convenient distance below this drawing mark another horizontal line to represent the centre line of the boat as seen in plan, and project on it the lengths of the deck and waterline. On each side of this centre line draw horizontal lines distant from it an amount equal to one half the breadth, in this case 1·8 inches on each side, and with these as a guide draw a plan of the deck and a curve for the L.W.L.

The next thing is to ascertain the sail plan, heights, position of masts and spars, position of deck erections and so forth. To do this from a sail plan, or proper drawing, is merely a matter of enlarging in correct proportion by the aid of dividers or with a specially prepared scale. When, however, the only available information is a few photos or pictures, and all of different scale, it is necessary to select one which depicts the boat broadside on such as the example in fig. 203, the *Sir Lancelot* reproduced from *China Clippers*, and to ascertain the chief dimensions from it, remembering that the picture may not show the vessel absolutely broadside or "flat on" but only approximately so, and if a photograph, there will inevitably be a certain amount of lens distortion which will adversely affect the matter. The simplest way to take off the position and height of masts, etc., is to make a scale like the one in fig. 204 based on the actual lengths of the L.W.L. on the photograph and the actual L.W.L. length on the drawing. Suppose these are 3 inches on the photo and 20½ inches on the drawing, the scale is then made as follows. Draw a horizontal line *A B* on a piece of smooth white card: and at right angles to it draw the parallel lines *C D* and *E F*, the latter spaced about 6 inches apart. The line *C D* will be used for the scale for the photograph, the line *E F* for the actual dimensions to be transferred to the drawings under construction. On the line *C D* measuring upwards from *A B*, set off a distance equal to the L.W.L. on the photograph, in this case 3 inches, and on the line *E F*, measuring again from

A B set off the L.W.L. length on the drawing, in this example $20\frac{1}{2}$ inches. Now divide each line *C D* and *E F* into the same number of spaces, say for example ten, thus the line *C O* will have ten spaces of 3/10 inches, while the corresponding spaces on the line *E F* will be a trifle over 2 inches. Join up the divisions by diagonal lines and number or letter them in any convenient way, and if desired subdivide them as much as is

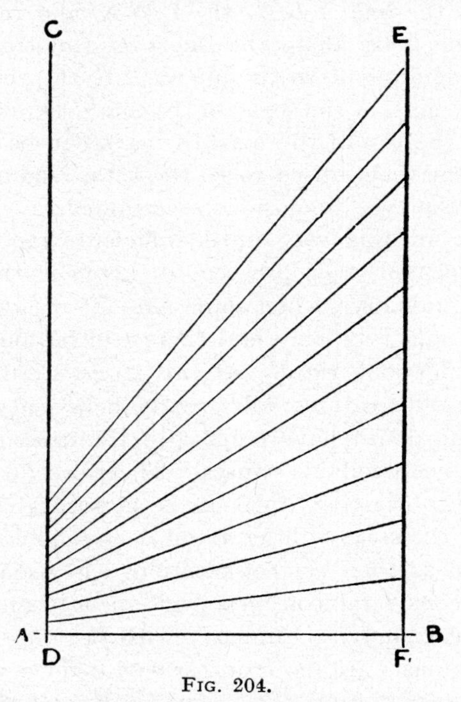

Fig. 204.
Special Scale for Measuring Photographs or Drawings.

reasonably possible. Now cut the card accurately along the lines *A B*, *C D* and *E F*. To use the scale always measure from the line *A B* to the desired part; for example, apply the line *A B* to the stern of the boat as seen on the photo, with the line *C D* parallel to the waterline. Note where the main-mast comes; as for instance, suppose it is opposite the 6th division, then run the finger along the diagonal line from this division to the edge *E F* and apply that edge of the scale to the drawing, with the line *E F* parallel to the L.W.L., and the line *A B* in register with the stern, then mark on the drawing opposite the 6th division on the line *E F* the position for the mainmast. Other particulars are taken in the same way as for example by applying the scale vertically to the photo, with the line *A B* on the L.W.L. and reading off the height of the mast along the line *C O* and transferring the corresponding amount on the line *E F* to the actual drawing. Should the length of the scale on the line *C D* not be sufficient to reach to the top of the mast, a mark can be made on the photo and the scale raised to it, the total reading then being the sum of the two dimensions ascertained.

Continue in this way until sufficient important points have been located, then proceed to sketch in the outlines of masts, sails and stays, when some amount of adjustment and a little give and take here and there will be found necessary to make things look right. At this stage a critical study of all available illustrations will greatly help matters, as some errors will no doubt have crept into the drawings due to a variety of uncontrollable causes. Therefore do not hesitate to amend the drawing until it is as accurate as possible. The lines of the stays will be found very reliable as checks to the drawing, as their correct positions can usually be determined with considerable accuracy and mast height or positions adjusted accordingly. Similarly with the yards, their positions on the masts are more or less well defined and should of course be so located on the drawings even if their position, as determined by the scales, appears to be somewhat different; the errors are mostly due to inaccuracies in the scale and distortions in the photograph.

However, a drawing prepared in this way will provide a far better working basis for a model than merely making it by eye, but of course such a drawing can seldom be more than approximately accurate.

FIG. 205.—*Port Jackson.*

The lines of the hull cannot be determined from the photographs and must be prepared in the regulation way as if making a new design. Fortunately, there are several reproductions of original lines of clipper hulls in existence and a number have been reproduced, for instance the book *Log of the Cutty Sark* contains the hull lines of *Cutty Sark* and also a sail plan; *China Clippers* gives the lines of *Thermopylae, Fiery Cross, Staghound, Flying Cloud, Lord of the Isles* and *Leander.* Thus these two books alone give examples of clippers from 1853 to 1869, and others are to be found in other books, museums and private collections, and possibly from the actual shipbuilders.

The sail plan is far more difficult to find and recourse has mostly to be had to photographs and designs. The latter will probably be the most serviceable as they often show the yards in an impossible position parallel with the centre line of the ship. An example (reproduced by permission from *The China Clippers*) is the *Sir Lancelot,* which could be scaled off as before described in a fairly satisfactory manner.

The most useful photograph of a clipper is the one taken bows or stern on, with the yards squared, as it is then possible to ascertain the proportions of the yards; as for instance fig. 205, *Port Jackson,* reproduced from *Colonial Clippers.* An intermediate scale can be made with one set of figures on the line *C D* for the first photograph, and those on the line *E F* for the second. Readings can then be compared between the two pictures and any ascertained from the second can be immediately translated on the first scale, as any point on the line *E F* on the second scale would still have as equivalent the corresponding point on the line *E F* on the first scale, because on both scales the basic divisions on the line *C D* are the same.

By careful and thoughtful use of available illustrations it is therefore possible to prepare sufficient drawings for all practical purposes of the ship-modeller, but it is in this respect, perhaps, more than any other branch of the work that practical experience and knowledge are necessary to attain the best results.

The novice is counselled to adhere to published drawings and data, leaving the evolution of special designs to those who specialise in such work, at least until a certain measure of competence has been attained.

FIG. 206.

The *Torridon.*

A few books, all inexpensive, which will be found useful to the ship-modeller, are mentioned on next page, but the list is by no means exhaustive neither does the omission of a book in any way infer that it would not be of utility; nor on the other hand that the following books are essential to the ship-modeller, although it is highly desirable to acquire or study as many works and illustrations of clipper ships as circumstances permit, such as the *Torridon,* fig. 206, reproduced from the *Log of the Cutty Sark.*

Bibliography

Masting and Rigging the Clipper Ship and Ocean Carrier. By H. A. Underhill. £3·30

Plank-on-Frame Models. By H. A. Underhill. Vol. I, Reprinting. Vol. II, £2·00

Sailing Ship Rigs and Rigging. By H. A. Underhill. £2·00

The Last of the Windjammers. By Basil Lubbock. Vol. I, £3·70 Vol. II, £3·70

The Log of the Cutty Sark. By Basil Lubbock. £3·50

The China Clippers. By Basil Lubbock. £2·50

The Colonial Clippers. By Basil Lubbock. £2·70

Dictionary of Sea Terms. By A. Ansted. £1·37½

INDEX